Seek

A WALK THROUGH THE PSALMS

PSALMS 61-90

by

KRISTIN SCHMUCKER

Study Suggestions

Thank you for choosing this study to help you dig into God's Word. We are so passionate about women getting into Scripture, and we are praying that this study will be a tool to help you do that. Here are a few tips to help you get the most from this study:

• Before you begin, take time to look into the context of the book. Find out who wrote it and learn about the cultural climate it was written in, as well as where it fits on the biblical timeline. Then take time to read through the entire book of the Bible we are studying if you are able. This will help you to get the big picture of the book and will aid in comprehension, interpretation, and application.

• Start your study time with prayer. Ask God to help you understand what you are reading and allow it to transform you (Psalm 119:18).

• Look into the context of the book as well as the specific passage.

• Before reading what is written in the study, read the assigned passage! Repetitive reading is one of the best ways to study God's Word. Read it several times, if you are able, before going on to the study. Read in several translations if you find it helpful.

• As you read the text, mark down observations and questions. Write down things that stand out to you, things that you notice, or things that you don't understand. Look up important words in a dictionary or interlinear Bible.

• Look for things like verbs, commands, and references to God. Notice key terms and themes throughout the passage.

• After you have worked through the text, read what is written in the study. Take time to look up any cross-references mentioned as you study.

• Then work through the questions provided in the book. Read and answer them prayerfully.

• Paraphrase or summarize the passage, or even just one verse from the passage. Putting it into your own words helps you to slow down and think through every word.

• Focus your heart on the character of God that you have seen in this passage. What do you learn about God from the passage you have studied? Adore Him and praise Him for who He is.

• Think and pray through application and how this passage should change you. Get specific with yourself. Resist the urge to apply the passage to others. Do you have sin to confess? How should this passage impact your attitude toward people or circumstances? Does the passage command you to do something? Do you need to trust Him for something in your life? How does the truth of the gospel impact your everyday life?

We recommend you have a Bible, pen, highlighters, and journal as you work through this study. We recommend that ball point pens instead of gel pens be used in the study book to prevent smearing. Here are several other optional resources that you may find helpful as you study:

• www.blueletterbible.org This free website is a great resource for digging deeper. You can find translation comparison, an interlinear option to look at words in the original languages, Bible dictionaries, and even commentary.

• A Dictionary. If looking up words in the Hebrew and Greek feels intimidating, look up words in English. Often times we assume we know the meaning of a word, but looking it up and seeing its definition can help us understand a passage better.

• A double-spaced copy of the text. You can use a website like www.biblegateway.com to copy the text of a passage and print out a double-spaced copy to be able to mark on easily. Circle, underline, highlight, draw arrows, and mark in any way you would like to help you dig deeper and work through a passage.

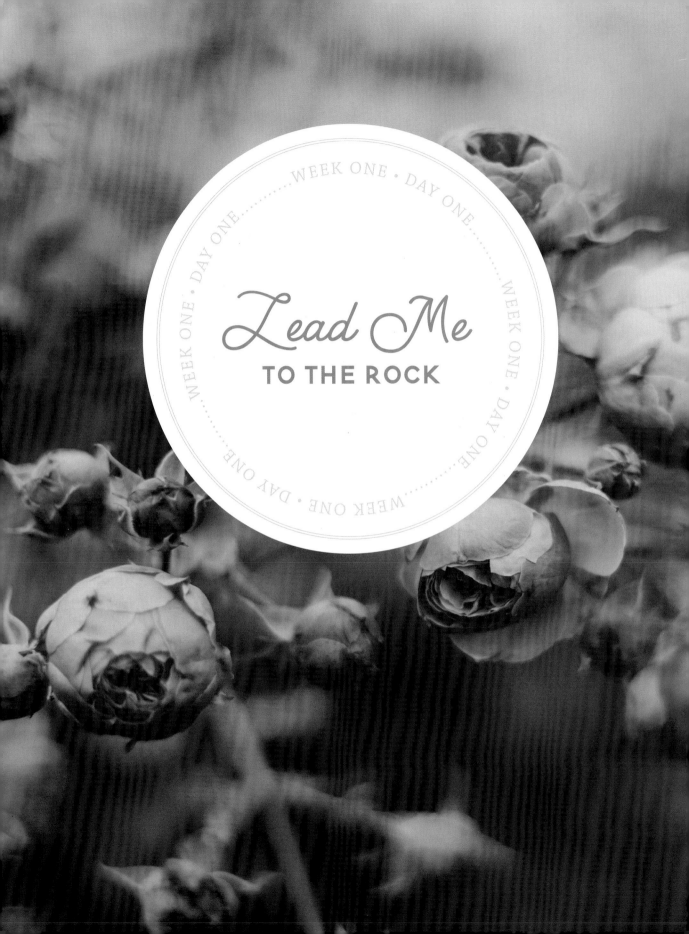

WEEK ONE · DAY ONE · WEEK ONE · DAY ONE · WEEK ONE · DAY ONE · WEEK ONE · DAY ONE ·

Lead Me
TO THE ROCK

PSALM 61

The trials of life can seem to overwhelm our souls, and yet for the child of God, His enduring presence pulls us back to Him again and again. This psalm of David encourages our hearts and instills in us a confidence that there is nothing that will separate us from His ever-present love. The psalm is one of longing for God. It is a psalm of personal lament and prayer, and also of confidence in God and the coming King.

The psalm begins with the persistent pleading of the psalmist. In the trials of life there is a desperation that is felt for God to hear. The trials that David faced did not push him away from the Lord – instead they caused him to pray and plead with God all the more. He prayed for God to hear him. Verse two shows us the position of the psalmist. He is described as being at the ends of the earth as he calls upon the Lord. In his fleeing from Absalom, he would have been far from Jerusalem at the end of the kingdom. Though this was a poetic exaggeration it shows us the emotions that we experience when trials are upon us. It is not uncommon to feel as though one is far from home, far from where we should be, or even far from the presence of God. The heart of the psalmist is weary, and yet despite the way that he is feeling, he knows where the answer for his sorrow lies.

The answer for our suffering and sorrow is not found within ourselves, but in the One who has created us. So the psalmist pleads to be led to the rock that is higher than I. He knows that there is one who does not grow faint or weary, and it is God alone who will give Him the strength that is needed to carry on. David does not simply plead for God, but also to be led to God. We not only need Him, but we need Him to get to Him. He is the author of our salvation and the hope for our weary souls. And when we are feeling as though we have no strength, we can rest in the truth that while that is true, we are anchored in the One whose strength is over and above all.

David uses beautiful imagery to help us get a small glimpse of who God is. He is our rock, our refuge, our strong tower and protector. He is our dwelling place and shelter is found in His wings. As David pleads from his distress, he chooses to focus not on simply what he is feeling, but on who God is. This is the basis of our prayers and the answer to our problems —the person, character, and glory of God.

When we look to ourselves, our strength, and our emotions, we will be disappointed. But when we look to our God, we will be assured of His presence and His character. In verse 4, we are pointed to God's presence as the psalmist speaks of the tabernacle and his longing to dwell in the tent of God forever. He seeks refuge in the shelter of the wings of God which is a symbolic reference to the wings of the cherubim in the holy of holies. The destitute and hopeless are ushered into the presence of God. This is not by any strength of their own, but by His perfect goodness and gentle love. It is in the presence of God that our fears are washed away.

The final lines of the Psalm shift to a prayer for the king. Though in a small way this prayer would be a prayer for the immediate Davidic dynasty, its far greater fulfillment would be found in Jesus who is the culmination of the Davidic dynasty and the one who will sit on David's throne forever (2 Samuel 7). And it is through union with Christ that we experience the blessings of this kingship as we rule and reign with Him. Jesus is the King forever, so the psalmist will praise Him forever. Day after day forevermore we praise the One who has rescued us and redeemed us. In this short psalm we see the full range of human emotion, and yet it is God's faithful presence and eternal kingship that secures our eternal praise whether here on earth when suffering is present, or in the new heaven and new earth when all is made new and sin and suffering is no more. We have a good and faithful God, and we will praise Him day after day for all eternity.

FOR YOU HAVE BEEN A REFUGE FOR ME, A STRONG TOWER IN THE FACE OF THE ENEMY.

Psalm 61:3

Day One Questions

1. Can you think of a time or situation in your life when you identified with the psalmist's emotion?

2. Summarize the psalm below.

3. Which image of God stands out to you the most from this psalm and why?

WEEK ONE · DAY TWO · WEEK ONE · DAY TWO · WEEK ONE · DAY TWO · WEEK ONE · DAY TWO

I WAIT FOR

God Alone

For God alone my soul waits. This is the way that the psalmist begins this psalm of confidence. It is a psalm of confident waiting. It is a psalm in which truth is rehearsed to our hearts as the psalmist rehearses truth to his own heart. This psalm is a reminder of the unchanging character of God, and it is a reminder to us to rest in His sovereign and tender hand.

Alone, only, and truly are some of the translations used for the tiny Hebrew word *ak*. This small word occurs six times throughout this short psalm. It's presence reminds us of what matters most, and truly it reminds us of the only thing that matters. It is for God alone that our souls wait and trust. He is all that we need and all that we have, and in having Him we have all that we need. This truth defies our emotions. The opening line of this psalm is a recognition of the supremacy of God in our lives. There is nothing that we want and nothing that we need apart from Him.

We wait for Him in stillness. We confidently anticipate Him to work. John Trapp poignantly reminds that, "Waiting is nothing else but hope and trust lengthened." Our waiting hearts are far from passive, instead we are urged to actively wait and rest our hope on God alone. For He alone can comfort, heal, restore, and renew. So often we think that we are waiting for our circumstances to change or waiting on other people or even ourselves, but the psalmist reminds us that it is for God alone that we wait. We can wait with hearts that are still before Him because our waiting is not an instance for anxiety, but for confident hope in a God who is always faithful.

The psalmist affirms many things about the character of God. He is my salvation, my rock, and my fortress. He is the source of our salvation and the sustainer of our lives. He is our everything. The forces of evil prey on weakness and attack the vulnerable, but our God is one who does not despise the weak and the vulnerable. A bruised reed He will not break is the reminder of Isaiah 42:3 that is echoed in Matthew 12:20 of Jesus. He comes with grace and mercy for burdened souls.

As verse 5 begins the psalmist restates the opening themes of the psalm with even more confidence than before. He is not commanding himself to trust. He is preaching to his own heart the truth that God is all that he needs. The confidence seems to grow more and more. In verse 2, David stated that he would not be greatly shaken, but by verse 6 he drops the modifier and boldly states that he will not be shaken. It is through God alone that he finds the confidence to trust the Lord.

The psalm shifts again in verse 8 as David begins to encourage others with the truth that he has encouraged himself with. We can trust the Lord at all times—not just sometimes or in certain situations, but at all times. The call is for the people of God to come and pour their hearts out before the Lord. He is their only refuge and only Savior. Come to the Lord weary soul; He is pleased when you come and pour it all before Him.

As the psalmist closes, his final admonition is to trust in God alone. Our hope is not in money, or success, politics, or power. Our hope is in God and He will not fail His people or His plan. The weight of His glory is deep and rich and far surpasses the vanity of this life. He is worthy of it all, and all of our hope is found in Him.

TRUST IN HIM AT ALL TIMES, YOU PEOPLE; POUR OUT YOUR HEARTS BEFORE HIM. GOD IS OUR REFUGE.

Psalm 62:8

Day Two Questions

1. Read through the psalm again. Write down all the words and phrases used to describe God.

2. What does this psalm teach you about who God is and how He interacts with His people?

3. Paraphrase Psalm 62:8.

My Soul
THIRSTS FOR YOU

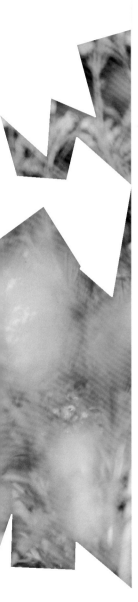

PSALM 63

It has been noted by many commentators that this is one of the most beautiful psalms in the Psalter. The psalm is most often thought to have been written by David while he was in the wilderness fleeing from Absolom. It paints for us in vivid strokes a picture of the glory of God, the beauty of His steadfast love, and our ever-present need for Him. Though it has elements of lament, it also has strong elements of confidence in the Lord and His love that is better than life.

This psalm begins with addressing God Himself and a reminder of how personal our God is. He is not simply God, He is my God. The psalm overflows with the actions of the psalmist that are used to describe his desperation for God's presence. These verbs stand as a call for us as well to follow in the path of the psalmist in seeking the Lord above all things. The psalmist seeks for the Lord earnestly and diligently. His soul thirsts for God. In the culture, the word for soul was used to denote the entire and complete being of a person. It is as though the psalmist speaks of thirsting for God with all that he is and every part of himself. The concept of thirsting for God is not isolated to the poetry of this psalm. Isaiah 55:1 sends out a call to all who thirst to come and drink, and in the New Testament, Jesus Himself would claim to be the living water (John 4:13-14, 6:35). The thirsty soul finds satisfaction in God alone.

Longing, fainting, or yearning for the Lord are also present in the psalm. And the end of verse one makes clear the condition in which the psalmist writes. As David looked around, he would have very literally seen a dry desert land, so it seems natural that he would recognize that the state of his location was also the state of his own soul. He found himself far from home and far from the sanctuary of worship. Yet he thinks back and remembers the glory of God that He has seen. He has seen the beauty of the Lord and He clings to that truth. The personal God of verse one, is also the majestic, holy, and glorious King.

In verse three we are pointed to the steadfast love of God. This is His hesed love that is seen so often throughout the Old Testament. It is His unfailing, covenant-keeping, pursuing, steadfast love. This love is better than all that life has to offer and even better than life itself. The statements that follow can be connected back to this declaration of

God's love. Because of this love, the psalmist will praise. Because of this life, the psalmist will bless the Lord and lift up His hands. The psalmist continues, but the words in verse five provide for us an important contrast. My soul will be satisfied. This satisfaction that is found in the Lord alone stands in contrast to the thirsting, fainting, and longing of verse one.

David clings to what he knows to be true. Because of who God is and because of His steadfast love, the people of God will be satisfied in Him despite our circumstances. He is truly better than life, so we can desire Him above all other things and know that we will always be satisfied. It may not be in the way that we anticipated, but we will be filled. We will behold His glory.

David speaks of the watches of the night. These changes of the guard would happen throughout the night, and David gives us the impression that he is awake for everyone of them. Yet, he transforms those sleepless nights into nights of worship. When the night is long and lonely, we can turn our gaze to Heaven. Hidden in His shadow, we will sing with overflowing joy.

We cling to Him as He holds fast to us. Like a child we grip the arms of our Father, yet it is Him that holds us up. The psalm ends with a declaration of the justice that will come. Rejoicing will come. Truth will reign. God will be praised. Our hearts are left longing for the day when the joys of this psalm will be fully known. We long for the day when full restoration is seen in the new heavens and new earth. We ache for the day when all of our longings will be fulfilled in Him, when our enemies will be defeated, and when we will dwell in His presence and behold His glory forever.

MY LIPS WILL GLORIFY YOU BECAUSE YOUR FAITHFUL LOVE IS BETTER THAN LIFE.

Psalm 63:3

Day Three Questions

1. Read through the psalm again and mark or write down every verb or action word that is attributed to the psalmist.

2. How does this psalm describe the Lord?

3. How does the description of the Lord transform the way that we look at our own lives?

WEEK ONE • DAY FOUR

Hear my Voice

Psalm 63 and Psalm 64 are often thought to go together. While Psalm 63 focuses on who God is in the midst of the attacks of the psalmist's enemies, Psalm 64 shifts the focus to look a little closer at the enemies and how God will ultimately bring justice and vindication for His people. Though the psalm does not contain a specific description as to the setting, it is often assumed to also take place while David was fleeing from Absalom, but the depth of emotion and frustration allows us to see our own struggles in the poetic words of the psalmist.

The psalm opens with the pleadings of David for God to hear, preserve, and hide him. As we journey through the psalms, we are struck with the way that David constantly turns to the Lord. Prayer is the place that he runs, and he always finds comfort, hope, and refuge in the presence of the Lord. David was an imperfect man, and yet he is an example for us of a man that returned to the Lord again and again. David knew his own weakness, and even in the moments that he didn't understand, he trusted in the Lord's strength to save.

If biblical scholars are correct in placing the writing of this psalm while David was fleeing from Absalom, David would have been facing real swords and arrows that sought to destroy him. Yet David sees that these physical weapons are symbolic of the spiritual battle around him. In Psalm 63, David saw the dry and weary dessert as a picture for his own soul, and here he sees the weapons that come against him as a picture of the words of his enemies that seek to destroy him not just with literal swords and arrows, but with lies, slander, and deceit.

The end of verse 5 speaks the fear that so often runs through our thoughts in light of the enemies of God in this world. Why does it seem that injustice and evil are not punished? Here the words are spoken by the evildoers themselves. They think they are getting away with their evil and sin. And from a cursory glance it does sometimes seem that way. We see many of God's people suffer, and we see some wicked men that seem to prosper. But things are not always what they seem to be. And as the psalmist continues, we will see his confidence in the love of God for His people and in His sovereign justice. It may seem like wickedness is prevailing, but even that is under the sovereign direction of a loving Father who has never once abandoned His people.

It is God who comes to the aid and rescue of His people. He will bring about justice and vindicate the righteous. Sin always brings consequences, and as we near the end of the psalm, we see that it is God who carries out these consequences for the wicked. The consequences that were set in motion by the entrance of sin into the world in Genesis 3 are an integral part of the human story, but the story does not end with the consequences of sin and the judgment of God. The final verse of the psalm points out that the righteous rejoice in the Lord. The righteous here are the people of God. These are those who were once as evil as the wicked men that are spoken of in this psalm, and yet they have been redeemed. The righteousness that they bear is not a righteousness of their own, but the righteousness that they carry because they have been clothed in the righteousness of God.

Like the psalmist, we can rejoice in confidence before we even taste the victory of our enemy's defeat, because we have tasted the goodness of the Lord (Psalm 34:8). We have tasted His goodness and we are confident that He will be faithful to us.

"WE HAVE TASTED HIS *goodness*

AND WE ARE CONFIDENT THAT HE

WILL BE *faithful to us.*"

Day Four Questions

1. We have consistently seen David running to the Lord in times of trouble. What do you learn from the way David responds to suffering?

2. Have you ever felt that wickedness was not punished when it should be? How does this passage remind you to trust in God's plan?

3. Why can believers rejoice before they fully see their enemies defeated?

WEEK ONE · DAY FIVE · WEEK ONE · DAY FIVE · WEEK ONE · DAY FIVE · WEEK ONE · DAY FIVE · WEEK ONE · DAY FIVE

THE GLORY IS
Yours

The tone of the psalter shifts with this psalm as we come to several psalms dedicated to praise. Psalm 65 is a stunning song of praise that overflows from a heart touched by God's grace. It moves our hearts to worship and reminds us that we should be people that have been transformed by the grace of God and in awe of the glory of God. This is the song of the people of God – He is worthy of all glory, and it is our joy to glorify His name.

The psalm begins with a reminder that praise is due to Him. The psalmist speaks of praise in Zion and he is referring to the place of worship which was at the time located in Jerusalem. As we read through this psalm, we cannot help but notice that the psalm speaks constantly about what God has done. This psalm of praise and thanksgiving does not focus on the one declaring these truths, but on God alone. He alone is worthy of worship. The psalm speaks of who He is and all that He has done for His people. It speaks of how He has blessed His people. These blessings are not merely material blessings, they are covenant blessings that overflow from a covenant-keeping God.

It is the Lord who hears our prayers, and it is from Him, to Him, and for Him that all things hold together (Romans 11:36). It is God that provides atonement for the sin that separates us from Him. In the Old Testament this was seen through the constant animal sacrifices. For us as the children of God, we look back to the cross as the place where Jesus secured atonement for His people. It is atonement that allows us to draw near to God. It is not anything that we have done or could do, but it is Him alone that provides and secures our salvation and fellowship with Him.

He has chosen us to be His own before the foundation of the world. He has drawn us near through the power of the gospel. He has done what we never could. With irresistible grace He has made us sons and daughters. We are His because He has chosen us and drawn us to Himself (John 6:44, 15:16). He is the God of our salvation and we find satisfaction in Him alone. He is the hope of the world and there is no hope apart from Him.

We worship Him who is the Creator of all things. The greatest mountains and the strongest seas were made by His far greater and far stronger hands. We gaze upon a sunrise in awe or wonder at the majesty of the mountains, yet the creation itself calls us to something deeper and far greater. Creation calls us to shift our gaze and fix our wonder on the Maker of the most majestic mountains and of the most glorious sunrise.

The God that we worship, is the God who created, and He is the God who sustains. He holds all things in the palm of His sovereign and almighty hand. The sovereign Creator is also the gracious sustainer and the tender gardener of the Earth. He holds all things together (Colossians 1:16-17). What a reminder of our security in Him. Who He is compels us to praise and it compels us to trust.

His glory is seen in creation and all of creation sings His praise. The earth has been wounded by sin, and yet it still points to the Lord. The earth yearns for renewal, and yet it worships while it waits (Romans 8:19-22). This is our story as well. Though we feel the impact of the fall, we worship while we wait for the day when all will be made right. Along with all creation, we will worship while we await the day of the Lord.

It is He that pursues, He that redeems, He that provides, and He that sustains. And it is He that we worship. We need a vision of God's glory to set in perspective the mundane and the magnificent. We need to know who He is to feel the depths of sorrow and the heights of joy. All creation praises Him and we join their song. He is worthy of all glory.

YOU ESTABLISH THE MOUNTAINS

BY YOUR POWER; YOU ARE ROBED

WITH STRENGTH.

Psalm 65:6

Day Five Questions

1. Read through the psalm again and mark or record every verb/action that is attributed to God.

2. What do you learn about God's character from this passage?

3. Take a moment to slowly go through the psalm again and pray the words of this psalm of thanksgiving back to God.

Week One

MEMORY VERSE

God, you are my God; I
eagerly seek you. I thirst for
you; my body faints for you
in a land that is dry, desolate,
and without water. So I gaze
on you in the sanctuary to
see your strength and your
glory. My lips will glorify you
because your faithful love is
better than life.

PSALM 63:1-3

Read Psalms 61-65

PARAPHRASE THE PASSAGE FROM THIS WEEK.

WHAT DID YOU OBSERVE FROM THIS WEEK'S TEXT ABOUT GOD AND HIS CHARACTER?

WHAT DOES THE PASSAGE TEACH ABOUT THE CONDITION OF MANKIND AND ABOUT YOURSELF?

Week One

HOW DOES THIS PASSAGE POINT TO THE GOSPEL?

HOW SHOULD YOU RESPOND TO THIS PASSAGE?

WHAT IS THE PERSONAL APPLICATION?

WHAT SPECIFIC ACTION STEPS CAN YOU TAKE THIS WEEK TO APPLY THE PASSAGE?

WEEK TWO · DAY ONE

Come and See

PSALM 66

Psalm 66 continues in this string of psalms that overflow with praise. This psalm is a call to praise the true and living God. It is a reminder of who He is and all that He has done. The psalm progressively narrows its focus, beginning first with a call to praise directed toward the entire earth, then narrowing to the people of God, and eventually narrowing to just one individual that is assumed to be the psalmist.

The first verses of the psalm give a rapid-fire list of the things that every person should be doing in praise to the Lord. The praise and worship here are directed at the glory of God and even the praise we are to attribute to Him is to be glorious praise. We along with the chorus of all creation worship Him for all that He is and all that He has done. All glory is due to Him alone.

Then the psalmist shifts his attention to the people of God. The people of Israel had seen God work mightily and gloriously on their behalf, and now the call to worship is a call to remember. The call goes out to the nations to come and see what God has done as Israel declares what He has done on their behalf. The Lord's works are awesome and good. This song of praise begins to recount the faithfulness of God. We are transported back to one decisive moment of deliverance as the people crossed the Red Sea on dry land. They escaped the bondage of Egypt and rejoiced for all that God had done. The Exodus is one of the most critical moments in all of the Old Testament, and it is one that Scripture constantly looks back to. And as magnificent as the Exodus from Egypt was, it was pointing all along the way to a greater exodus and another decisive moment in history. The Exodus points us to the cross. It points us to the moment when our slavery to sin was broken forever, when our enemies were destroyed, and when we were graciously delivered by the sovereign hand of God. Remembering our redemption must always lead us to worship.

God had daily sustained His people, but the journey had not been without struggle. After that victorious deliverance the people found themselves sojourning in the wilderness. It should not come as a surprise to us, that the New Testament refers to our own lives with the same language of exiles and strangers in a world that is not our home.

The psalmist points out that it was the Lord who had allowed the testing; it was Him that had allowed them to face hardship and suffering. At first this may confuse us and leave us wondering why God would be active in both the deliverance as well as the struggle. From our earthly perspective we may not understand, but God in His sovereign wisdom knows what is best for us when we do not. He knows that it is often the testing and the struggle that molds us into who He has called us to be. The testing is just as significant as the triumph. Both are carefully guided by His hand. And in fact, 1 Peter 1:7 will remind us that the testing of our faith is what refines us and ultimately brings praise and glory to God alone.

Through the fire and through the flood (Isaiah 43:1-2), God is present and working in a million ways we may never understand until we see Him face to face. The language of verse 12 reminds us of the crossing of the Jordan into the promised land. The people went through the water to be brought to the promised land. Abundance was not a result of their hard work, merit, or ease – it was a gift from God.

The psalm narrows once again to speak of one individual believer. While Israel declared come and see to declare the works of God to the nations, the psalmist says, come and hear to tell what God has done for his own soul. What at first seems like a decrescendo from the earth, to the nation, to the individual is actually a crescendo declaring personal and intimate love of God. The God that created the world and is owed all praise, also delivers His people, and knows each one of His children by name. The God who receives the praise of a thousand sunsets also hears the prayer of you and me. He has loved us. How can we help but praise Him.

COME AND SEE THE WONDERS OF
GOD; HIS ACTS FOR HUMANITY
ARE AWE-INSPIRING.

Psalm 66:5

Day One Questions

1. How does remembering cause us to worship?

2. Why do you think that the seasons of testing are just as important as the moments of deliverance? What does God teach us in times of testing? In times of deliverance?

3. Why is it important for us to remember that God is God of the earth, of His people, and of us as individuals? How does that compel us to worship?

LET THE NATIONS
Be Glad

This psalm consists of just seven verses, and yet these verses overflow with praise to God. We do not know the author of the psalm or the specific situation in which it was written. Most scholars assume that it is a psalm that would have been sung during one of the harvest festivals. It is both prayer and prophecy—praying for the glory of God among the nations and looking forward to the day when the earth is renewed, and the nations will ascribe glory to the Creator.

The psalm first looks backwards and then looks forward. It reflects backwards to the Aaronic/priestly blessing that was given in Numbers 6:24-26. The famous words seek the grace and blessing of God and His face to shine upon us are nearly quotes at the start of the psalm. The theme of the psalm also reflects back to the Abrahamic covenant found in Genesis 12:1-3 and the promise and commandment given to Abraham that he would be blessed in order to be a blessing. The people that sung this psalm would have recognized that same calling in their own lives. The abundant blessings of God should always propel us to share what God has done and invite others into the blessing that we have received.

As the people of God we desire the presence of God and the psalmist and Aaron poetically state this as the desire for God's face to shine upon us. The words remind us that the glory of God changes us. Just as Moses' face shines after encountering God's glory (Exodus 34:29-35), we are transformed into the image of God by the glory of God (2 Corinthians 3-4). Here in Psalm 67 we see a chain reaction beginning. It begins with God's glory and ends with God's glory because this is the principle goal of all things. The presence of God among the people of God leads to the proclamation of God's glory and the praise of God among the nations.

The desire of the people of God is for the glory of God to be known and the praise of God to ring out from every tribe, tongue, and nation. The mission is never to seclude ourselves in an "us vs. them" mentality. Instead, the "us" is compelled to go to "them" so that they may be part of "us." When we go to the nations, we are imaging God who has pursued us and uses us to pursue His people around the world.

The hope of the nations is not found in politics or development. It is not found in technology, economics, or infrastructure. The hope of the nations is Jesus. And so the praise of the nations being given to God is both our mission and our prayer. It is what we pray for just as the psalmist writes in this psalm and it is what we dedicate our lives to.

And we go in confidence, knowing that it is God who goes with us and in us. We go and we do the work, but the Lord is the one who brings the harvest. We proclaim the message of the gospel, but it is God who is drawing His own and imprinting gospel-hope on the hearts of people around the world.

God has been gracious to us. He has blessed us. Now we must dedicate our lives to making Him known and trust that He will accomplish it. And someday in the new heavens and new earth we will praise our God forever with believers from every tribe, tongue, and nation.

LET THE PEOPLES PRAISE YOU, GOD;

LET ALL THE PEOPLES PRAISE YOU.

Psalm 67:3

Day Two Questions

1. Summarize the message of Psalm 67.

2. How does the glory of God change the people of God?

3. How does our redemption compel us to share the message of salvation with the nations? How can we practically do this?

THE GOD WHO
Triumphs

This is a psalm of triumph and a song of victory. It is quite a bit longer than the other psalms we have looked at and yet throughout its stanzas, it recapitulates praise to God alone. This psalm of David is thought to have been written when the ark was being moved from the house of Obed-Edom to the city of David. It was a moment of triumph for the people as they looked back to all that God had done, rejoiced in the moment of what He was doing, and also looked forward to the great things that He would do. The psalm was also traditionally sung at the feast of Pentecost/Weeks as a harvest song to praise the name of the Lord.

The first words of the psalm echo back to Numbers 10:35. And if this psalm was written to celebrate the moving of the ark, David repeats the words of Moses in the book of Numbers from when the ark first set out on its journey. The psalm does not resign itself to just one style. As we read, we can feel that the psalmist is bursting with worship at every turn. Words do not seem adequate enough to praise the Lord for who He is and all that He has done. The psalm goes between prayer, praise, thanksgiving, and adoration. It is a call to worship the God who has delivered His people, the God who is delivering His people, and the God who will deliver His people from every tribe, tongue, and nation.

Throughout the psalm we see the action of God. He is delivering and fighting for His people. And we see the actions of the people of God. They are rejoicing, worshiping and praising the Lord their rescuer. The name of God is mentioned throughout the psalm and it points us to the fact that God has revealed Himself to His people. He has revealed Himself and it is that revelation that emboldens our courage to trust Him to do what He has said that He will do.

Verses five and six contain some of the most beautiful descriptions of God. He is the powerful warrior, yet He is also the One that bends low to those who are helpless and needy. He is the everlasting God, and He is also the Father to the fatherless. He is the conquering King and yet He also sets the solitary in homes. It is a description of who God is and also a description of the kind of people that He is calling us to be. We image God when we care for orphans and protect widows. In fact in the book of James, we are told that this is true religion (James 1:27). This is who He has called us to be.

As the psalm continues, the psalmist looks back at the ways that God has moved and worked in the lives of His people. The words of the psalm look back to the Exodus, the entrance into the promised land, and a great part of the psalm echoes the words of the song of Deborah that is found in Judges 5. This middle portion of the psalm places great emphasis on how God has faithfully delivered His people in the past.

Beginning in verses 19, we see a shift. The psalmist had praised God for what He had done, now He praises God for what He is doing with confidence that He will do it again in the future. As the people of God, we rejoice in past, present, and future deliverance. We know that our future deliverance is just as certain as the deliverance we have already tasted. As the psalm ends, we see that the audience has grown from the immediate audience of the people of Israel on a certain day in history to the nations of the world praising God. We are called to worship with this same vision. We do not only praise for the past or even for the present. We praise God by remembering who He is and what He has done for His people, we rejoice in what He is doing, and we fix our eyes on Jesus and look ahead with steadfast hope because we know that He will do great things. What more can we do but praise the One who was, who is, and who is to come.

BLESSED BE THE LORD! DAY AFTER DAY HE BEARS OUR BURDENS; GOD IS OUR SALVATION.

Psalm 68:19

Day Three Questions

1. Read through the psalm again and mark or record the actions of God in the passage. What does this teach you about God?

2. Read through the psalm again and mark or record the actions of man in the passage. What does this tell you about how we should respond to the Lord?

3. After reading this passage, write a summary of how God is described in this passage.

PRAISE IN THE
Darkness

This is a psalm of praise in the darkness. Though it chronicles for us the sufferings of the psalmist and points us to the sufferings of our Savior, it does this while focusing on the praise of God from His people and from all of the earth. He is worthy to be praised. He is worthy to be praised in our joy and worthy to be praised in our suffering. We can rejoice because of the very thing that this psalm points to. The psalm repeatedly points us forward to the cross and this deepens the meaning of the beautiful and poetic words of David. The psalm is one of the three most quoted psalms in the New Testament and it is overflowing with words that point us to our Savior.

The psalm begins with the state of the psalmist. He has found himself in deep waters and overwhelming suffering. He is hated and slandered by those around him. He is weary and waiting. Yet despite his many enemies that wrongly accuse him, in verse 5, he remembers his own sin. He knows that he is a sinner in need of God's mercy and grace. And though many of his accusations are false, he knows that he is still a sinful man. The immediate response of the psalmist is not self-preservation or to fight back with slanderous words for his enemies. His concern is for the people of God and for the glory of the name of God. He does not want his life or his sins real or imaginary to bring shame on the name of God or the people of God. And in verse 9, we are told that he is consumed with zeal for the house (and assumed worship) of God. We see in his response a lesson for ourselves on how we should respond with humility to the suffering that we face.

The psalmist response to suffering is to run to the Lord. And yet, we do not see him pleading his case and appealing to God on the basis of his own work or character. He does not come to try to convince God that he is a good man and does not deserve what he is facing. Instead, he comes to God and appeals to Him on the basis of God's character and God's work. The appeal is not that the psalmist was a "good" person and not deserving of this injustice, but that God is a good God. We come to God on the basis of who He is and the steadfast truth that we are His. Our deliverance is not hinged to our goodness, but to His.

Beginning in verse 19, the psalmist continues to speak of the things that he is facing. As he speaks to God, he says, "You know." God knows the things that we are facing, because Jesus has already faced them for us. Reproach, shame, and dishonor were placed on Jesus for us. He took on our sin though He was sinless so that we could partake in His radiant righteousness (2 Corinthians 5:21). The psalmist uses poetic language and metaphors to portray the way that he feels in his sufferings, but the things that he describes are a foreshadowing of the things that Jesus faced in reality. The words describe for us in many ways the events of the crucifixion and the treatment of Jesus in his earthly life and ministry. The sufferings that we face have been faced by Jesus before us and we cling to the promise that just as we suffer with Him, we will also be raised with Him (2 Timothy 2:12). We rest in this unshakable promise

The psalm ends in what may seem to us as an unexpected way. The psalmist does not close with frantic petition for his own condition, but with praise for God alone. It is God who is the hope of his people. It is God who is worthy of all glory. It is God who will bring His sovereign plan to pass. It is God who is good. And it is God who we will worship no matter what this life may bring.

"IT IS GOD WHO WE WILL

worship no matter what

THIS LIFE MAY BRING."

Day Four Questions

1. Have you ever experienced the emotions of this psalm? How so?

2. What do you learn about who God is from this psalm?

3. What enables believers to praise in the midst of suffering?

O LORD, MAKE
Haste

PSALM 70

This psalm of David is cited for the memorial offering. It is thought to have been sung as a prayer for God's blessing on His people and it is nearly identical to Psalm 40:13-17. It is a personal lament and a prayer for justice, and yet it is also a psalm in which the psalmist is reminded of his own need for the Lord and reminded of the goodness of God through all situations.

The psalm opens with the cry of the psalmist to God. Make haste or hurry begins the psalm and shows the urgent and bold prayer of the psalmist. He is seeking the blessing and aid of God almighty and He boldly asks God to answer Him quickly. The entire psalm is an urgent and bold prayer from the heart of the psalmist to the ears of God.

The psalmist pleads for justice to reign. He asks for God to help His people and defeat the enemies that rise up against the people of God. This is not a selfish prayer. The psalmist is pleading for God to be true to His character and all that He has promised to be for His people. The psalmist is praying what Jesus prayed in the Lord's Prayer, "Your kingdom come, Your will be done." This is not a prayer of petty requests, but a prayer for the kingdom of God to push back the darkness of sin and evil in this world.

And yet even in the midst of this warrior prayer there stands a reminder of the truth. In the midst of the urgent prayer for God's immediate help comes a prayer for the rejoicing of God's people. The psalmist prays that all who seek the Lord will rejoice and be glad in Him alone. He rejoices that those who love salvation and the God of salvation can say unceasingly that God is great. These words are a reminder to us to worship no matter what circumstances surround us. The people of God can forever say that God is great when things are good and when our circumstances weigh down our hearts and our days. This truth remains that He is good. The people of God are never without hope because the God of hope is always good.

The final verse of this brief psalm is a reminder of our poor and needy status before the Lord. We are in desperate need of our God. We need Him for every moment and for every breath. It is Him who is our help and our deliverer. It is He who sustains us. We have no power to save ourselves and we have no power to change our circumstances, and yet we can rest our lives in the hands of the One that has power over not only our lives and our circumstances, but over all things. We are secure in the grip of His grace. We are sustained with the assurance of His goodness.

We stand on the other side of the cross as we look back to this psalm. As the people of God we have union with Christ and the Spirit of God dwelling within us. We have a Comforter that is nearer than a brother and we have union with the King of Kings. Though poor and needy sinners, if we have been saved by His grace, we have been made the heirs of God. And though this life still brings trouble and trials, is there any greater reason for rejoicing than for all that God has done for us? We are His and we need not fear what this life will bring.

I AM OPPRESSED AND NEEDY;

HURRY TO ME, GOD.

YOU ARE MY HELP

AND MY DELIVERER;

LORD, DO NOT DELAY.

Psalm 70:5

Day Five Questions

1. Have you ever experienced a time when you prayed a prayer asking God to hurry with an answer?

2. Paraphrase Psalm 70:4.

3. What attributes or character traits of God do you see in this psalm?

Week
Two

MEMORY VERSE

Let all who seek you
rejoice and be glad
in you; let those who
love your salvation
continually say,
"God is great!"

PSALM 70:4

—— Read Psalms 66-70 ——

PARAPHRASE THE PASSAGE FROM THIS WEEK.

WHAT DID YOU OBSERVE FROM THIS WEEK'S TEXT ABOUT GOD AND HIS CHARACTER?

WHAT DOES THE PASSAGE TEACH ABOUT THE CONDITION OF MANKIND AND ABOUT YOURSELF?

Week Two

HOW DOES THIS PASSAGE POINT TO THE GOSPEL?

HOW SHOULD YOU RESPOND TO THIS PASSAGE?

WHAT IS THE PERSONAL APPLICATION?

WHAT SPECIFIC ACTION STEPS CAN YOU TAKE THIS WEEK TO APPLY THE PASSAGE?

WEEK THREE • DAY ONE...... WEEK THREE • DAY ONE...... WEEK THREE • DAY ONE...... WEEK THREE • DAY ONE

Continual

PRAISE

Psalm 71 is one of the few psalms without a heading. And though we do not know the psalm's author with certainty, it is usually assumed to be a psalm of David due to many similarities with other psalms of David. The psalm is classified as a personal lament, and yet the psalm expresses a range of postures. It is filled with lament, with petition, and with worship, all of which is overflowing with thanksgiving to the Lord. Though we don't have many details about the psalm, there are several phrases in it that have led commentators to believe that it is written by a person that is older or even elderly. It is a psalm of looking back on one's life and knowing that God has been faithful every step of the way, and He will be faithful to preserve us until the end.

The psalm begins with the psalmist declaring that it is in the Lord that he takes refuge or finds protection. Where else is there for the child of God than the refuge of the God who rules all things. The righteousness of God that once condemned us in our sin is now the hope that we cling to. The child of God has been clothed in the righteousness of Christ (2 Corinthians 5:21), and we rest in the justice and righteousness of our loving Father.

As verse three opens, the psalmist petitions for God to be a rock of refuge. Interestingly, we see here a different Hebrew word than was used in verse one. While the word in verse one has the meaning of protection, this word in verse three means habitation or home. God is our protection and deliverer, and yet he is also our habitation and shelter from both our enemies and from all things. Our habitation is found in Him and it is to Him that we continually come and find rest.

Though the psalmist faces difficulty throughout the psalm, we continually see him returning to the truth that he will praise God in and through every situation that he faces, and when his life is drawing near the end he will still look back and praise God for His faithful provision through every season, every suffering, and every moment. As the children of God, our hope is not in the shifting sands of our circumstances. Our hope is in the steadfast and immovable character of our God. Even if everything around us changed, He would remain faithful and ever the same.

And because of this steadfast faithfulness, we can praise Him in and through every situation. We can rejoice in hope that is unshakable and count even our trials as joy (Romans 12:12, James 1:2). There is no day in the life of the believer, no matter how dismal it may appear, that the child of God cannot worship. Verse 14 points out that the praise is continually growing more and more. Our praise of God should increase with every day and every moment as we know Him deeper and see His hand more clearly, until the day when we see His face and our earthly praise gives way to perfect worship forevermore.

God walks with His people through every moment of this life. From the child in the womb to the aging saint, God's care is present and sure. In verse 20, the psalmist recognizes that perfect sovereignty of God that had caused him to face troubles and yet sustained and revived his soul through it all. We have this same confidence. He will go with us. The streams of His mercy will never come to an end, and we will never cease to praise Him for His faithful love.

BUT I WILL HOPE CONTINUALLY

AND WILL PRAISE YOU

MORE AND MORE.

Psalm 71:14

Day One Questions

1. Look up the words refuge and habitation in a dictionary. What do they mean, and how do you see that meaning in God who is our refuge and habituation?

2. The psalmist makes a point to speak often in this psalm about praising God continually. Why do you think we should praise God continually?

3. What does this psalm teach you about God? What does it teach you about our response to God?

WEEK THREE • DAY TWO

FOREVER
King

What makes a good king? This is the question that we are faced with as we approach this beautiful royal psalm. This psalm is attributed to Solomon and is a description of the kingship. Though it would have had an immediate fulfillment in the Israelite kingship, its ultimate fulfillment would come in the King of Kings. In fact, in the Jewish Targum, the word Messiah was added in the first verse to show that it was recognized that this was a psalm that was pointing to the Messiah. For only He could fulfill the role of the perfect king.

In 2 Samuel 7, we are introduced to a kingly line that would come from David. It is there that we find what is known as the Davidic covenant. It is a covenant made by God to David. It is a promise that the son of David will sit on David's throne forever. In Solomon, David's son, we see an immediate and partial fulfillment. Solomon would sit on the throne of David, build the temple, and continue the Davidic line. But Solomon was not an everlasting king. Someone else would have to fill that role.

This psalm speaks of the many characteristics of this perfect king. He is righteous, strong, and compassionate. He proclaims truth, and cares for the needy. This king brings peace and flourishing to the people of God. He reigns in a kingdom that is not just within the boundary lines of Israel, but to the ends of the earth. Kings and nations bow before him. Though he is powerful and mighty, he lifts the head of the needy and oppressed. He redeems those discarded by society and brings growth and abundance to His people. His name endures forever and ever.

Though Solomon in a partial and immediate way could fulfill some of these things, he could not be the perfect king. Though Solomon spoke words of wisdom and righteousness, his life and actions were consumed with chasing after his own passions and lusts. Though he was a wise judge in the nation, his wisdom and judgment in his personal life fell woefully short of the picture presented in this psalm. Though he conquered and reigned, he still died, just as every mere human does. Solomon in all of his greatness and all of his splendor simply served to point to a greater king.

The greatness and splendor of this king can only be seen in the face of Jesus. Rabbis and ancient hymn writers were right to read this psalm and see Jesus. This psalm sings the praises of His glory, and stirs our hearts to do the same.

Jesus is our perfect and forever king. He is righteousness. He is the embodiment of wisdom and our perfect judge. In active obedience, He lived the perfect life that we could not live. He conquers the powers of sin and hell and reigns forever and ever. And this king that formed the earth with the power of His Word, is alive today. The power of death could not hold Him in the grave. He is the greater king that our hearts long for.

And I wonder if just maybe our hearts were made to feel a twinge of anguish over our earthly kings. Earthly kings at their worst show us the depravity of human hearts, and at their best they still can not measure up to a heavenly king. We need a greater king, and His name is Jesus.

This psalm and the second book of the psalms ends here with a benediction. It is a prayer of praise and worship for the true King. As we read these words, may our hearts echo this prayer. May the whole earth be filled with His glory. May His kingdom come.

BLESSED BE THE LORD GOD,

THE GOD OF ISRAEL, WHO

ALONE DOES WONDERS.

Psalm 72:18

Day Two Questions

1. Read through the psalm again. Write a description of the king that is described here.

2. Read Revelation 21:22-27. How do you see Psalm 72:11 fulfilled in this verse?

3. Read the benediction of Psalm 72:18-20 again. Paraphrase the prayer of praise below in your own words.

Jesus Shall Reign

by ISAAC WATTS

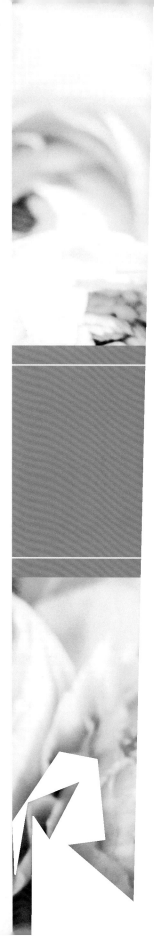

Jesus shall reign where'er the sun
Doth his successive journeys run;
His Kingdom stretch from shore to shore,
Till moons shall wax and wane no more.

To Him shall endless prayer be made.
And princes throng to crown His head,
His name like sweet perfume shall rise
With every morning sacrifice.

People and realms of every tongue
Dwell on His love with sweetest song;
And infant voices shall proclaim
Their early blessings on His name.

Blessings abound where'er He reigns:
The prisoner leaps to lose his chains,
The weary find eternal rest,
And all the sons of want are blest.

Where He displays His healing power
Death and the curse are known no more;
In Him the tribes of Adam boast
More blessings than their father lost.

Let every creature rise and bring
Peculiar honors to our King;
Angels descend with songs again,
And earth repeat the loud Amen.

WEEK THREE · DAY THREE ..... WEEK THREE · DAY THREE · DAY THREE ..... WEEK THREE · DAY THREE · WEEK THREE ..... DAY THREE · WEEK THREE

Truly

GOD IS GOOD

This psalm begins the third book of the psalms and is the first psalm written by Asaph. It is generally titled as a wisdom psalm and features themes reminiscent of the books of Proverbs and Job. While the previous psalm begged us to ask the question of what makes a good king, this psalm also prompts a question to rise deep in our being. Is God good? The question churns in our minds and resembles answering a question from a catechism. The psalm begins with the declaration of the goodness of God to His people. The first verse states what may have been an early creed and a declaration of faith in God's good character.

Yet the abiding truth of God's ever-present goodness almost seems to be overshadowed by the anguish of the verses that follow. While the psalmist acknowledges God's goodness in the first verse, he describes his own state in the verses that follow. He is stumbling and envious. He is discontented with his life and jealous of the seeming prosperity of the wicked. As the psalmist looks around, he sees that the wicked are abounding in wealth, health, outward beauty, and are living lives that seem to be devoid of any problems. But the psalmist's description of the wicked initially ignores some key aspects of their lives. This is what envy does to us. It spreads through our hearts and minds and makes us think that there is something better on this earth than what we have been given. Envy is not only a poison that rushes through our veins, it is also an accusation against the character of God. When we are envious of others, we are accusing God of not being good.

When we finally reach verse 17, we learn of the one thing that shifts the perspective of the psalmist, and it is the worship of a holy God. Worship shifts our gaze off of ourselves and on to the Lord. As we look up from ourselves and gaze upon Him, we see the light of His glory break through the bleakness of our present circumstances. Anguish is transformed into adoration in the presence of God.

The psalmist thinks of the end of the wicked. Though it may seem that they have all things at this moment, they do not have the thing that matters most. They are far from God and living with a faux peace that is a far cry from the peace of God. Just as was the psalmist, we are in need of an eternal view and not a temporal one. We need to seek the things that are above, and not the fleeting things of this world (Colossians 3:1). As verse 23 begins we see how the psalmist's perspective is changing. He recognizes the constant presence of God, and sees God's actions in the present, the immediate future, and the ultimate future. God will hold our hands, guide us, and ultimately receive us into glory. God will finish what He has started. These declarations remind us of the promises of Romans 8:29-30; our salvation is secure from beginning until end. He will do what He has promised.

As the psalm draws to a close, we see that as the psalmist shifts to adoration; he has recognized that God is the greatest desire of all. We do not consider neither wealth or fame, nor power or beauty to be our prize. This is what is valued in the eyes of the world. God is our prize. Without Him we have nothing, but we have everything in Him. Duty is transformed into delight in the presence of God. The psalm that began with truth spoken out of duty, but mixed with the anguish of human experience is transformed into a heart that delights in God in the midst of those experiences. The creed or confession is no longer just academic knowledge, but truth that has been experienced.

The truth triumphs over our feelings. This is the message of Psalm 73. So we must preach the truth back to our own hearts. We must cling to what we know to be true of God, even when our circumstances would tempt us to question His goodness. May we rehearse His goodness like a liturgy of the heart, and a constant reminder of His unsurpassed goodness.

WHO DO I HAVE IN HEAVEN BUT YOU?

AND I DESIRE NOTHING

ON EARTH BUT YOU.

Psalm 73:25

Day Three Questions

1. What truths do you learn about God's character from this passage?

2. What truth do you need to preach to your own heart when your circumstances threaten to overwhelm you?

3. What passages of Scripture bring comfort in seasons of struggle. Make a list here to reference.

WEEK THREE · DAY FOUR ...... WEEK THREE · DAY FOUR ...... WEEK THREE · DAY FOUR ...... WEEK THREE · DAY FOUR ......

YET MY GOD IS

Working

Psalm 74 is a lament psalm, and more specifically it is a corporate lament. It is a psalm that reflects on the destruction of the temple, and seems to point to the destruction of Jerusalem that took place during the Babylonian invasion. Yet the emotions and truths that are expressed in this psalm are timeless. This psalm points a sorrow-filled people to the hope that is found in Christ alone.

The psalmist surveys his situation and asks why God has abandoned His people. The situation was bleak. The temple had been destroyed and with it seemed to vanish the hope of Israel. The temple was more than a building for worship. It was a symbol of the presence of God among His people. It was the dwelling place of God on earth. But the temple and the tabernacle before it were but a picture that pointed toward a far greater spiritual reality. The temple of God that symbolizes God's presence in the midst of humanity pointed to the temple that is Jesus Himself who took on a tent of human flesh to dwell in the midst of the people that He came to save. Jesus is the true and better temple.

Just as the temple of this psalm was destroyed by the Babylonians, the temple of Jesus seemed to be destroyed as well. As Jesus died on the cross, the hope of the disciples and followers of Christ seemed to vanish from their sight. But God was working in ways they did not see to fulfill His promises. Jesus rose from the grave three days later defeating death and conquering the grave. Now we as His people look forward to a day in the new heaven and new earth when there will be no need of a temple because God Himself will be in our midst (Revelation 21-22). And even now the body of Christ is the temple of God with the Spirit dwelling in the people of God.

In verse 9, we see the psalmist cry out in confusion. How many times have we faced similar experiences when we do not know what God is doing and the situation seems so hopeless? Yet in these moments, the answer is not to look at our situation, or to look at ourselves, but to look to our God. It is in seeing Him that our circumstances and ourselves begin to slip into focus.

Beginning in Psalm 74:12, the psalmist changes the tone of the psalm and begins to speak of the truth of who God is. His words remind us of the truth of God's character in the midst of bleak situations. The psalmist looks to the past and recounts the steadfast faithfulness of God for generations from parting the Red Sea to creating the world. He looks to the present and knows that God is King and He is presently at work in the world for His glory and the good of His people. At the end of the psalm, he speaks of the present while also looking to the future. He pleads with God to be faithful again just as He has always been.

This psalm gives us a glimpse into the anguish of the exile and the hope that is found in Jesus who has come as a true and better temple. It encourages us to pray in light of the character and faithfulness of God. It reminds us that God is faithful and He is faithful to His covenant. He has done what He has said that He will do and He will always do what He has said that He will do. And even when our situation doesn't make sense and our surroundings seem hopeless, we can trust that He is already working to bring about His perfect plan.

THE DAY IS YOURS, ALSO THE

NIGHT; YOU ESTABLISHED

THE MOON AND THE SUN.

Psalm 74:16

Day Four Questions

1. Can you think of a situation in your life when you felt like God had forgotten you?

2. How did you respond? How is remembering who God is a better response?

3. Write down some past, present, and future truths about who God is to encourage you through a difficult season.

PRAISE TO THE GOD
of Justice

This psalm of Asaph is a thanksgiving psalm. It is a psalm of corporate worship that reminds us of all that God has done, and of His holiness and justice. It is a psalm that causes us to remember His grace and thank Him for who He is.

The psalm begins with the congregation speaking praises and thanksgiving to God. The people praise God for who He is as expressed in His covenant name. They give thanks because God is near. He is not detached and far off from the people that He has made. And they remember and recount all that God has done. The people needed to remember what God had done, and this act of remembering would instill in their hearts trust for His present and future faithfulness.

As the psalm continues there is a shift and the words give us insight into the work of God in this world. We see here the balance between God's sovereign action and man's human responsibility. God is sovereign over every moment of our lives, and at the same time man is responsible for their actions.

God in His holiness will not let wickedness continue forever. He will punish evil. Yet the words of this psalm call us to trust in His sovereign plan as we are reminded that He will judge evil at the set time. When the world seems like it is falling apart, it is our God who is holding it together. The lyrics to the children's song is true—He has the whole world in His hands. What a reminder for us not to try to hold it in our own hands.

The only thing that we can boast in is in the Lord. This is made plain in the verses of this psalm. It is the Lord who lifts up and the Lord who puts down. The words of the psalm echo the words of Hannah's prayer of praise to the Lord in 1 Samuel 2, and they also draw our minds to the Magnificat of Mary before the birth of Jesus. The psalmist along with these two women recognized the important truth that we have no power in ourselves. We cannot make ourselves powerful, wise, or wealthy. We cannot raise ourselves to a position of prestige or pull ourselves up by our own bootstraps. And there is no such thing as a "self-made man."

Instead, all that we have is from the Lord who has made heaven and earth and who holds every star in place. As He rules the world with His sovereign hand, He guides our lives and the events of the world with tender care. And though sin and evil seems to infect this world's every molecule, every molecule is under His sovereign command. And there will come a day when He will judge evil and rid this world of sin's consequences. A new heaven and new earth are coming that will abide within God's perfect order. We wait for that day with eager and expectant hearts.

The wrath and judgment of God against sin is likened to a cup in this psalm. This illustration is one seen throughout the Old Testament in numerous places (Isaiah 51:17, Jeremiah 25:15, Hebrews 2:16). This imagery is not isolated to the Old Testament though. In Matthew 26:39-42 we see Jesus in the garden prepared to take the bitter cup of God's wrath in place of His own people. As the people of God, the wrath of God that we deserved is swallowed by the Son of God in our place. This is the essence of the gospel. The substitutionary atoning work of Christ is what enables us to not fear His righteous judgment, but to instead rest in His sovereign care. Jesus has taken the wrath of God that we deserved and now we enjoy the blessings of righteousness because we are clothed in His righteousness.

As the people of God, we will sing His praises forever because He has been abundantly faithful to us.

FOR GOD IS THE JUDGE:

HE BRINGS DOWN ONE

AND EXALTS ANOTHER.

Psalm 75:7

Day Five Questions

1. Read 1 Samuel 2:1-10 and Luke 1:46-55 and record any similarities between the message of this Psalm and Hannah and Mary's prayers.

2. How does God's righteousness give us hope?

3. Read Matthew 26:39-42. Why is it significant that Jesus took the cup of God's wrath in our place?

Week
Three

MEMORY VERSE

My flesh and my heart may fail, but God is the strength of my heart, my portion forever.

PSALM 73:26

Read Psalms 71-75

PARAPHRASE THE PASSAGE FROM THIS WEEK.

WHAT DID YOU OBSERVE FROM THIS WEEK'S TEXT ABOUT GOD AND HIS CHARACTER?

WHAT DOES THE PASSAGE TEACH ABOUT THE CONDITION OF MANKIND AND ABOUT YOURSELF?

Week
Three

HOW DOES THIS PASSAGE POINT TO THE GOSPEL?

HOW SHOULD YOU RESPOND TO THIS PASSAGE?

WHAT IS THE PERSONAL APPLICATION?

WHAT SPECIFIC ACTION STEPS CAN YOU TAKE THIS WEEK TO APPLY THE PASSAGE?

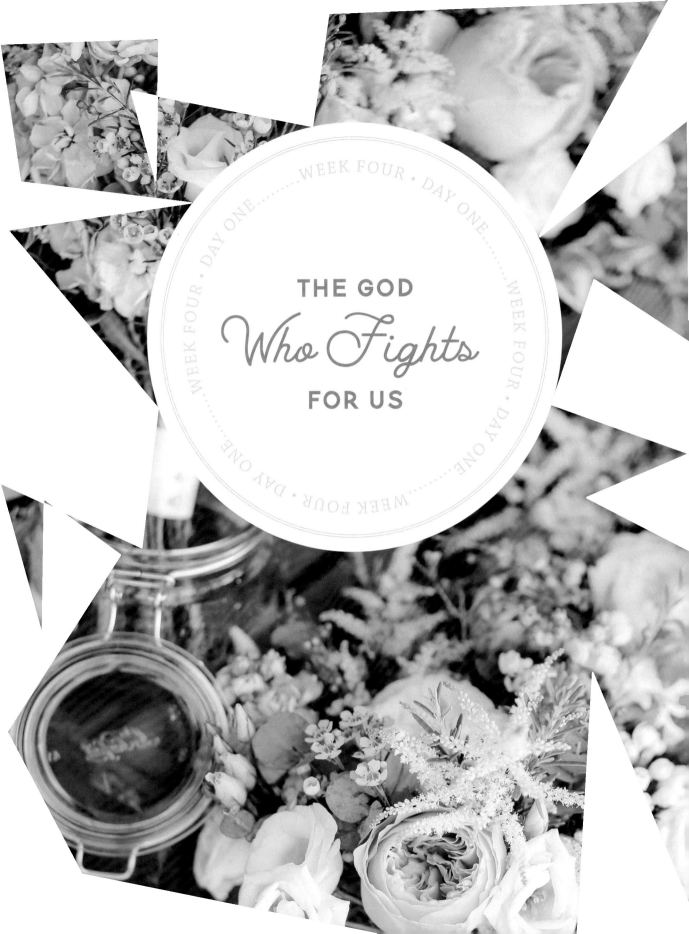

WEEK FOUR · DAY ONE

THE GOD
Who Fights
FOR US

This psalm of Asaph is a psalm about our God who fights for His people. This psalm is believed to have been written as a response to the defeat of the army of Sennacherib (Isaiah 37:33-36). It is a reminder of God's powerful working in the lives of His people. God is zealous for His own glory and zealous for the good of His people. He is strong and mighty and a warrior that fights battles and defeats our enemies.

The opening line of the psalm begins with a reminder that should encourage our hearts. God makes Himself known to His people. Pause and think about that magnificent truth. Though we will never fully comprehend everything that He is or understand everything that He does, we can know God. He desires us to know who He is. And yet this knowledge is even more than just knowing about God, though that is a good thing. Not only can we know about Him, but we can also know Him and be in relationship with Him.

Yet the Lord who is known to His people, is also the protector and passionate defender of His people. Verse two speaks of His abode or dwelling place, and the Hebrew words here are used elsewhere to describe the den or lair of a lion (Jeremiah 25:38). Our God is both lion and lamb. He is the God who we can personally and intimately know and He is the God who fights our battles. And if our God is for us, we can be assured that nothing and no one could ever stand against us (Romans 8:31-39). Our greatest enemies and strongest foes are no match for our all-powerful God.

We see in this psalm that our God is greater than the greatest armies and stronger than the strongest weapons of warfare. At the end of verse five, we see a striking phrase that tells us that the men of war were unable to use their hands. These words give us a compelling picture of the scope of God's power and sovereignty. Try as they might, humanity will not be able to stand against God's plan. They will be rendered useless in battle and they will only be able to go as far as God allows them to go.

As we come to the final stanza of the psalm in verses 7-10, we are reminded that it is God alone that we should fear. There is no other fear for the people of God than the fear of God. And the fear of God silences all other fears. We can have confidence that there is no one that can stand against His plan. God will judge in righteousness at the appointed time, and that judgment will be the defeat of evil and the ultimate salvation of God's people. Verse 10 points out that even the rebellion and sin of mankind will serve God's purposes as it fulfills His plan and displays His mercy. These words though perplexing to us are not a contradiction, but a beautiful paradox. This is the foundation of passages of Scripture like Romans 8:28 and Genesis 50:20 that remind us that even the bad things in this life will be used and transformed in God's sovereign plan for the good of His children and the glory of His name.

This should compel us to a greater trust in our God. The God that is known to us, also fights our battles, and the God that fights our battles will win those battles and use every moment of our lives for His glory. We see this beautifully displayed in the cross of Christ where God used the wickedness of men and their crucifixion of Jesus to bring salvation to the people of God. Acts 2:23 demonstrates beautifully for us how God in His sovereign plan used the lawless actions of the men that crucified Jesus to fulfill the definite plan of God foreknown since before the world began. What a comfort for us. What an encouragement to trust Him. He is fighting for us and He will not abandon us.

AT YOUR REBUKE, GOD

OF JACOB, BOTH CHARIOT

AND HORSE LAY STILL.

Psalm 76:6

Day One Questions

1. What does it mean that God can be known? How should that truth encourage us to study God's Word?

2. How is God described in this psalm?

3. How does this psalm encourage you to trust God?

Preaching
THE GOSPEL
TO OURSELVES

This psalm of Asaph is one in which the deep agony and desperation of the human condition is expressed. Yet the psalm is also one in which we are compelled to remember the goodness and deliverance of God. This psalm is one that encourages us to preach the gospel to our own hearts throughout our lives. The structure of the psalm is divided into two parts. The beginning section gives us a clear picture of the emotional anguish that we so often experience, and the ending section of the psalm compels us to put our hope in God alone, to remember His deliverance, and to trust His unseen hand.

Many people wrongly believe and teach that there will be no troubles or sorrows for the children of God. However, this is just not seen in Scripture. Throughout the Bible, we see God's people walk through deep suffering, and Jesus Himself is our example of suffering with our hope placed firmly in God. So we should not be surprised by the range of emotions expressed in Psalm 77. The psalmist is expressing for us an inward struggle to trust and seek the Lord.

The psalmist cries out to the Lord and seeks Him through the distress of this life. When the psalmist looks around at his life and sees his situation, he is tempted to despair. His situation seems hopeless and though he is trying to seek the Lord, he does not understand what God is doing, or why He has allowed the circumstances of his life.

Yet at the start of verse 10 there is a shift. While the first verses of the psalm focuses on self, the psalmist shifts his perspective and looks to the Lord. He looks to the Lord and He remembers. He remembers what God has done for His people and He remembers who God is. He remembers, and he meditates. He allows his mind to be more consumed with the character of God than with the circumstances of his life. When his thoughts are shifted to the Lord, it seems that words of praise begin to flow from his lips. His attention has been shifted off of himself and on to the Lord.

The psalmist looks back to the Exodus and God's deliverance of His people from the bondage of Egypt. And the psalmist finds hope in this single and decisive event and monument of deliverance. With vivid language he describes how God rescued and redeemed His people from bondage. He remembers how God is stronger than anything that comes against Him from the powers of evil, to the powers of nature. In all of this remembering, he is encouraged to trust God in his own situation. He is reminded that as verse 19 reminds us, God's footprints are sometimes unseen.

This is encouragement to us today. It encourages us to follow the example of the psalmist and preach the truth of the gospel and the goodness of God to our own hearts when we are tempted to not trust the Lord through the sorrows of this life. It encourages us to be reminded of who God is and look at our lives in light of the overwhelming truth of His goodness.

And just as the psalmist looked back to one decisive event in the history of the people of God, we can look back to one decisive event as we look to the cross. It is through the cross that we can be assured that the powers of evil and the powers of earth have no power over our all-powerful Savior. Jesus has conquered, and Jesus is reigning. We find our greatest hope as we fix our eyes on the cross and remember the gospel. But our human hearts are prone to forget, so we must preach the gospel to our hearts each and every day. We must remember who He is and how He has delivered His people.

YOU ARE THE GOD WHO WORKS WONDERS; YOU REVEALED YOUR STRENGTH AMONG THE PEOPLES.

Psalm 77:14

Day Two Questions

1. Paraphrase the message of Psalm 77.

2. Why do we need the gospel even after we have been saved?

3. What do you think it means to preach the gospel to yourself in everyday life? How can you practically do that this week?

YET THE LORD
Is Good

We have come to Psalm 78. This psalm of Asaph is the second longest psalm in the Psalter behind only Psalm 119. This psalm combines many different elements to form a unique psalm. It contains aspects of wisdom literature and poetry. It is ultimately a history lesson turned heart lesson. While the history of the nation of Israel is being recounted from the Exodus to the kingship of David, the psalm is didactic. It is meant to teach important truths about humanity and about who God is. This is so much more than mere historical facts; it is a lesson in the character of God in the face of our sin and weakness.

The psalm is presented as a lesson and a parable. The psalmist poetically tells of the history of the nation. He spends time highlighting certain aspects such as the Exodus and the wilderness wanderings to prove some very important points. The psalm tells us about a wayward, rebellious, and sinful people, and about a steadfast, unwavering, and compassionate God. Though the people rebel time and time again, God has not forsaken His plan.

In verse 18, we see the people testing God and doubting His goodness. This is not something new. As early as the first sin in the garden of Eden, Adam and Eve were questioning God's ways and wondering if He would do what He had said that He would do. We are not exempt from this same struggle. We wonder if God's Word and His law are truly good for us. We wonder if we are missing out on something. We struggle to trust His sovereign plan. In verse 19, the people ask the question, "Can God spread a table in the wilderness." This question in its immediate context referred to God's physical provision for His people. Yet the question goes much deeper than that. It is the question in the heart of every person about the goodness and provision of God. Will He do what He has said that He will do?

Yet throughout the Psalm we see God's faithful provision. We see words and phrases like, "yet, in spite of all of this, and despite" that remind us that God was ever faithful to His Word and to His promises. He did what He had promised despite the fumbling, stumbling sins of the people. Through it all, God was still working to bring about His perfect plan to rescue and redeem His own. And no amount of sin and rebellion could change that eternal plan.

Verse 38 gives us beautiful insight into God's eternal character. Despite everything that the people had done, He was ever compassionate. He atoned for their sin and in mercy, He did not destroy them. He extended mercy and grace to people that did not deserve it.

Yet despite all that He had done, many rejected Him. They worshipped idols, they did not keep His Word, and they tested and rebelled against Him. But the psalm does not leave us without hope. And in fact it reminds us that our hope is not in other people, and our hope is not in ourselves. Our hope is in God alone. The end of the psalm is a promise of what God will do and how He will use David. The psalms end with promises of a temple and a shepherd.

The steadfast character of God has never changed. And this psalm in all of its beauty was pointing us to an even greater fulfillment in One that was still to come. We saw that God is compassionate, atoning for sin, and full of grace and mercy, and this pushes us to the cross. It is there that once for all God made atonement for the sins of His people through the sacrifice of Jesus. While we were rebellious, He came. While we were yet sinners, He died (Romans 5:8). We were chasing idols and looking for anything that would satisfy, and He was chasing us and bringing to us a satisfaction that is only found in Him. The temple is fulfilled in Jesus who is God with us. And Jesus is the Shepherd of our souls. And all of the promises to David are fulfilled in Jesus alone. The hope for our sin-sick hearts is the One who has steadfastly loved and pursued us.

"WHILE WE WERE REBELLIOUS,
HE *came*. WHILE WE WERE
YET SINNERS, HE *died*"

Day Three Questions

1. Summarize the message of Psalm 78 in one sentence.

2. What actions do you see the people doing in this psalm? What actions is God doing in this psalm?

3. Based on man's actions and God's actions in this psalm, what do you learn about God and man?

WEEK FOUR • DAY FOUR • WEEK FOUR • DAY FOUR • WEEK FOUR • DAY FOUR • WEEK FOUR • DAY FOUR • WEEK FOUR • DAY FOUR • WEEK FOUR • DAY FOUR •

How Long,

O LORD?

How long, O Lord? This is both the title of the psalm and a question found within Psalm 79. This psalm of lament, which is written by Asaph is often considered to be a companion psalm to Psalm 74 which also dealt with the same events of the fall of Jerusalem to the Babylonians. Though the psalm does lament the events of the destruction of the holy city, it is also a lament over the sins of the people that caused this destruction to take place. It was the sin and the rebellion of the people that had caused God's judgment to come at the hand of the Babylonians. Whether the psalmist was present when the events took place or is looking back at a historical event years later, it is clear that he is deeply moved by the pivotal events that took place when Jerusalem fell.

How long, O Lord is also a question that we may ask as we look at the world around us. We ask this question as we pour out our hearts in prayer in regard to the sin and destruction around us, and also about the sin that is within us. We yearn with the apostle Paul and all of creation for the "revealing of the sons of God," and through it all we trust that the suffering of this life can not compare to the glory that will be revealed on that day (Romans 8:18-25).

This psalm is one of pleading and lament for deliverance from a problem that is the fault of the ones that are pleading. The psalmist along with the people of God plead for grace and mercy for God's people and they plead for judgment against evil. This is a paradox of God's people both pleading for God's justice, while not living in perfect justice. The pleading of How long, O Lord must then go deeper than asking for our present circumstances to be fixed. For the psalmist and those that would have originally sung and prayed these words, it must also be a cry for the Redeemer. Because it is only through Jesus that mercy and grace can come for a fallen and sinful people.

We read this psalm with a different perspective. We stand on the other side of the cross. We live between two advents. We have experienced the grace of the first advent, and yet we still await the perfection of our faith that will come with the second advent. We groan with creation and wait with the people of God for our King to return. We plead with God for justice and await the day that the sin around us will be defeated and the sin within us will be eliminated.

For now, we live pleading for God to sanctify us day by day and remove the sin that so easily besets us. We run to the cross over and over and remind ourselves of the power of the gospel. We come in confession and repentance knowing that if we confess our sins, He will lavish us in forgiveness and restoration (1 John 1:9).

The psalm ends with the praise of the people and with pleas for the glory of God's name. What a fitting end to this psalm as we pray it back to the Lord. Through every moment of our lives, we will praise Him. We will praise our Shepherd and live our lives to bring glory to His name. And we will look forward to the day when all sin and brokenness will be forever vanquished, and His glory will shine brighter than the sun.

GOD OF OUR SALVATION, HELP US—
FOR THE GLORY OF YOUR NAME.
RESCUE US AND ATONE FOR OUR
SINS, FOR YOUR NAME'S SAKE.

Psalm 79:9

Day Four Questions

1. Think about the world today. What are the things that make you think, "How long, O Lord?"

2. Look back to the companion psalm, Psalm 74. What similarities and differences do you see?

3. How are believers able to praise the Lord even through difficulty?

RESTORE US,
O God

Psalm 80 is another lament of Asaph, and yet it is also a pleading for restoration. Throughout the psalm the refrain of "restore us" rings out. In some ways it feels that the psalm looks around and sees the hopeless condition of the people of Israel, but it does even more than that. The psalm looks ahead to the coming Messiah who would be everything that Israel could not be, and everything that we cannot be. This psalm provides foundational concepts that through the progressive nature of Scripture will be fully revealed to us in the New Testament.

The psalm begins by speaking of God as the Shepherd of Israel. This designation is not unique to the passage. God is often described throughout the Old Testament as the Shepherd of His people. With an understanding of Shepherd as a name of God in the Old Testament we have a fresh understanding of the radical nature of Jesus' claim in John 10 to be the Good Shepherd. By claiming this title, He was claiming to be God in the flesh. And in the same chapter in John, Jesus would proclaim that the Shepherd lays down His live for the sheep. He knows His sheep and calls them by name. And for the Jewish listener these radical claims were the claims of a man claiming to be God Himself.

The psalm also mentions the shining face of God. It gives us reference to the Aaronic blessing in Numbers 6:25, and it also reminds us of the shining face of Moses who saw just a glimpse of the glory of God in Exodus 33-34 and his face shone from the reflection of God's glory. What was an isolated event in the Old Testament is not the present reality of believers on this side of the cross. 2 Corinthians 3:18 tells us that we stand with unveiled faces beholding God's glory, and it is that glory that transforms us into the image of Christ.

Throughout the second half of the psalm, one theme stands out and it is the theme of the vine. It is another theme that is not unique to this psalm. Throughout the Old Testament Israel is portrayed as a vine. And here we see that theme again as the psalmist speaks of the vine that has been brought out of Egypt, and planted in the land. God had carefully planted and cultivated the nation of Israel as His chosen vine. Isaiah 5:1-7 gives us perhaps the clearest picture of Israel as the vineyard. Here we see that they vineyard of Israel did not yield good grapes, but instead brought forth wild grapes. For all of God's goodness and tender care as the Master Gardener, this vine had rebelled. Isaiah's prophecy speaks of consequences for the vineyard and Psalm 80 proclaims the same tragedies. The walls of the vineyard have been broken down and the fields of this vineyard have been ravaged. The psalm ends with pleading to the Lord who is the Shepherd of His people and the one who has planted the vine to bring restoration to the vine.

The words of the psalm close in what seems a hopeless manner. What hope is there for the discarded vine. But in John 15, we see a new vision of a true and better vine. It is in John 15 that we are told that Jesus is the true vine. It is here that the people of God are called to abide in the true vine and through His power bear much fruit. It is here that we are reminded that without Him we can do nothing. We find the concept of the vine again in Romans 11:11-24 as we learn that through the power of the gospel, Gentiles can also be grafted into the true vine through the grace and mercy of God. Some branches were broken off so that we could be grafted in, and it is all made possible because of the grace of the Father who is the Vinedresser, the Son who is the true Vine, and the Spirit who helps us to abide in the Vine and bear much fruit.

RESTORE US, GOD OF ARMIES;

MAKE YOUR FACE SHINE ON US,

SO THAT WE MAY BE SAVED.

Psalm 80:7

Day Five Questions

1. In what ways is God our Shepherd?

2. Read John 15. How is Jesus the better vine?

3. How does Jesus enable us to abide and bear fruit?

Week Four

MEMORY VERSE

Then we, your people, the sheep of your pasture, will thank you forever; we will declare your praise to generation after generation.

PSALM 79:13

Read Psalms 76-80

PARAPHRASE THE PASSAGE FROM THIS WEEK.

WHAT DID YOU OBSERVE FROM THIS WEEK'S TEXT ABOUT GOD AND HIS CHARACTER?

WHAT DOES THE PASSAGE TEACH ABOUT THE CONDITION OF MANKIND AND ABOUT YOURSELF?

Week Four

HOW DOES THIS PASSAGE POINT TO THE GOSPEL?

HOW SHOULD YOU RESPOND TO THIS PASSAGE?

WHAT IS THE PERSONAL APPLICATION?

WHAT SPECIFIC ACTION STEPS CAN YOU TAKE THIS WEEK TO APPLY THE PASSAGE?

WEEK FIVE · DAY ONE · WEEK FIVE · DAY ONE · WEEK FIVE · DAY ONE · WEEK FIVE · DAY ONE

A CALL TO
Listen

Psalm 81 is another psalm of Asaph, but it does not seem to fit into the typical psalm categories. Instead, it is usually classified as a prophetic psalm or hymn. The words of the psalm have many of the same characteristics as that of the prophetic books of Scripture. It is likely that it was specifically written to be sung at one of Israel's many feasts. Most ascribe it to the Feast of Tabernacles or Weeks or the Feast of Trumpets. The psalm overflows with covenant language regarding God's covenant blessings for His people if they keep the covenant and of the covenant consequences if they do not. The psalm is also a reminder of God's tender love and provision for His people.

The psalm opens with jubilant praise to the Lord. This is a call for God's people to worship Him. Though the rest of the psalm will deal with difficult truth for the people to hear, these words ground the people in the beauty and glory of God and prepare their hearts to worship Him.

As the psalm continues, the psalmist grounds the psalm in the character of God and His mighty works for His people throughout their history. The God who speaks to His people today is the same God that cared for His people in the land of Egypt and delivered them out from the hands of their masters. He is the God who heard their cries and rushed in with deliverance. He is the God who answered them when they were in need. And He is the God who led them through the wilderness and tested them there. Through every step of the journey, He was there.

As verse 8 begins, the people are called to listen and to hear. The language reminds us of the famous Shema found in Deuteronomy 6:4 that every Israelite would have been familiar with. The people are called to follow one of the same commands brought down the mountain by Moses. They are to forsake all idols and have no god, but Yahweh. He is the One that has delivered them. The temptation of idolatry was one that Israel struggled with. The false gods of the nations were enticing to them. And they were always offering something that Israel thought that it needed. But the true God is the only one that satisfies. The people went chasing after idols, while their covenant Lord stood calling them to return and promising to fill them and satisfy their every need.

But Israel refused the covenant blessings of God that came with covenant faithfulness. Instead they chose the consequences of covenant disobedience. While the Lord stood with arms open wide, they ran to false gods that would bring them no lasting peace. While the Lord stood ready to defeat their enemies and conquer their foes, they chased after gods they could make with their own hands. Still the Lord stood pleading for His people to return, and pleading for them to receive the abundant life that only He could give.

Try as they might, Israel could not obey the Lord in their own strength. But Jesus would come as the perfect embodiment of the law. He would live the perfect life and follow God's law perfectly in the place of those He came to redeem from the bondage of sin. He came to bring a far greater deliverance than that of the deliverance from Egypt. And as Jesus walked the road to Calvary, He walked toward the moment when He would bear the sins of everyone who would believe. It is there that He would conquer the enemy of sin, by becoming sin for us. And abundant life is found only in Him. Satisfaction is found only in Jesus.

Yet so often we too chase after idols that will never satisfy, we run to things that bring temporary peace, when His arms are outstretched calling us to abide in the Vine and live in the strength that He alone provides. And He is faithful to call us back to Himself and for that we return to the opening verses of the psalm. For who He is and all that He does, we will praise Him all of our days.

I AM THE LORD YOUR GOD, WHO
BROUGHT YOU UP FROM THE LAND
OF EGYPT. OPEN YOUR MOUTH
WIDE, AND I WILL FILL IT.

Psalm 81:10

Day One Questions

1. This psalm reveals Israel's idolatry. How does idolatry sometimes take root in your own heart?

2. What aspects of God's character are revealed in this psalm?

3. What does this psalm call you to do in response?

Justice
TO THE WEAK

This is the second to last psalm of Asaph, and it is another that is can be difficult to classify. It has aspects of both corporate lament and prophetic hymn throughout the psalm. The psalm examines leaders that do not lead well, and makes us long for the leadership that God alone can bring.

The psalm begins and ends with a reminder of who our ultimate judge is. It is the Lord alone who judges, and it is the Lord alone who reigns.

The psalm speaks several times of the "gods" and this can be a challenge of interpretation. Several views have been set forth about who the psalmist is referring to. Some options include the principalities and powers seen in Ephesians 2, or the false gods of the people spoken of metaphorically. It seems most likely that the psalmist is referring to human rulers whether from within the people of Israel or from the nations that oppressed them. These gods that are named are condemned in the psalm and are not placed on the same level as the one true God.

The message that is given is that even human leaders are endowed with the responsibility of justice. They are commanded to help the weak and the orphan. They are to rescue the needy and the marginalized. The Lord charges governments and leaderships with a duty to protect the most vulnerable of society, but sadly throughout human history, leaders have failed at this task. Instead of protecting the weak, corrupt men have built up their own strength. Instead of rescuing the vulnerable, the outcast, and the orphan, leaders have discarded them to instead build up their own name and line their own pockets.

These cries for justice seem to echo the message of the prophetic books, and this is why this psalm is seen as prophetic. The psalmist calls out those that lack knowledge and wisdom and walk in darkness. But the psalm is also seen as a corporate lament because these despicable actions should be wept over, mourned, and lamented.

But the weeping, mourning, and lamenting must not last forever. And this psalm of sorrow is also a psalm of hope. Because there is a judge who is far greater than the judges of men. There is a ruler far greater than the corrupt rulers of Israel's day and of our own. There is one greater than the kings of the nations. He is the King of Kings and the King of all nations. His name is Jesus. He does not squelch the sick and the marginalized, but He heals them. He does not reject the poor, the vulnerable, or the sinner, but instead He calls them his sons and daughters.

This psalm is one of hope because even as we look at our flawed, and often evil, human rulers, we are being reminded of a better ruler. The rulers of the world fall short of the standard set by our perfect King. And the wickedness of human leaders makes our hearts yearn for the true King – The King of Kings.

And the psalm that is full of lament ends in victory and assurance. Because no matter what is happening on the world's stage, there is a day when Jesus will judge the Earth. The psalmist makes us long for that day. And for the original readers, his words left an aching for One that they did not yet fully know. It made them yearn for the man whom God has appointed to judge (Acts 17:31). For every human heart aching for justice to reign, we look to the Lord who forever reigns as our Just One.

"FOR EVERY HUMAN HEART ACHING FOR *justice* TO REIGN, WE LOOK TO THE LORD WHO FOREVER REIGNS AS OUR *Just One*."

Day Two Questions

1. How do human leaders make us long for Jesus who is our true and better king?

2. Why do you think we are tempted to trust in flawed human leaders?

3. Write out a prayer as you reflect on the Lord's righteous justice.

YOU ALONE ARE

God

Psalm 83 is the last of this collection of Asaph psalms. It is classified as a lament, but it is also one of the imprecatory psalms. It is a psalm of pleading with the Lord for justice for the people of God.

The psalmist pleads for the Lord to not be silent and to bring justice for His people. The psalmist rightly realizes that the sin of the enemies of God, while it impacts us, is first sin against the Lord. This is true of all sin, including our own (Psalm 51:2). Though sin has consequences and impacts people, all sin is first and foremost sin against the Lord. So the people that the psalmist speaks of are not simply the personal enemies of the psalmist, but the enemies of God and of truth and goodness.

We may feel shocked at the strong language of this psalm and of other imprecatory psalms, but we must understand that this is not a man in his flesh seeking for revenge or vindication. Instead it is a passionate plea for God's holiness and justice to prevail. The motivation of the psalmist is not personal glory, but the glory of God. The psalmist is pleading for the triumph of God's holiness over the evil activities of men. The psalmist is not trying to build his own kingdom, but God's kingdom. This must be true in our own lives as well, that we are seeking after the glory of God and His kingdom.

Though the start of the psalm focuses on God's holiness and justice, the final verses of the psalm also plead for God's mercy and compassion. The psalmist prays that the Lord would draw people to Himself, and that the wicked would turn to the Lord in repentance. He prays that the ultimate outcome would be the praise of the Lord and that all would know that He alone is God of all the earth.

How do we apply a psalm like this? It is important for us to realize that though we are now the people of God, we were once the enemies of God. Yet, while we were still sinners trapped in our sin with no way of escape, Jesus died for us (Romans 5:6-11). We were far from God and outside of His covenant people when Jesus paid the price for the sins of all who would believe. And the consequences of sins that are described in this psalm for the wicked, were placed not on us, but on Jesus Himself. He bore the weight of the wrath that we deserved and suffered in our place.

Jesus took our punishment on the cross and became our substitutionary atoning sacrifice so that we could be sons and daughters of God. Now we do not need to fear the justice and judgment of God. Instead we rejoice in His justice and righteousness, knowing that He will judge sin and evil will never prevail.

And we know that God will judge all sin and will one day vanquish evil, so we pray for Him to rescue and save sinners just as He saved us. And through it all we seek the glory of His name above all.

"WE REJOICE IN HIS JUSTICE AND RIGHTEOUSNESS, KNOWING THAT HE WILL JUDGE SIN AND *evil will never prevail*"

Day Three Questions

1. How does this psalm impact the way that we think about sin and evil in the world?

2. What do we learn about God in this psalm?

3. How does who God is bring us comfort in our everyday lives?

HOW LOVELY IS

Your

DWELLING PLACE

Psalm 84 begins a series of psalms that are attributed to the Sons of Korah. The Sons of Korah were those that David had designated to lead the people in songs of worship. In this psalm, we see a song written to be sung on the journey to Jerusalem to worship. This is a song of longing and celebration. It is a psalm that overflows with the love of God's people for the presence of God.

The psalmist begins with a declaration of how lovely is the dwelling place of God. It is not lovely because it is a beautiful building, but because it is the symbol of God's presence to His people. This is further seen as the psalm continues to speak of how the soul longs for God and for His presence. The heart and flesh, that is every part of us, longs for and sings the praises of the covenant God.

The place where God dwells is a place of blessing for those that dwell in it. Though the people of Israel would not have had full access to all parts of the temple, and though the holy of holies and the place where God dwells was accessed only by priests, they still loved and longed to be in the house of God. Their hearts yearned to be as close to God as possible. Nothing mattered more.

Yet, though the people longed to go to Jerusalem and to the place of God's presence, the journey was not an easy one. The pilgrimage would be long and hard and the people would walk through the driest of deserts before reaching Jerusalem. Yet in all of their overflowing joy even the desert would be a place of joy. And little by little and strength to strength they would be sustained through the journey by the Lord until they reached their destination. And eventually they would come to their destination where the lowliest position would be far greater than being anywhere else, and where blessing is found for those that trust the Lord.

Unlike the people of Israel when this psalm was originally written, we do not travel to Jerusalem to celebrate the feasts each year. And yet the words of this psalm are still applicable to us on this side of the cross. And in light of the cross, we experience a far deeper reality of these words sung so long ago. While the temple represented the dwelling place of God, because of Jesus, God now dwells in His people. And there is coming a day when time is no more and God will fully and finally dwell in the midst of His people and there will be no need of a temple because we will see Him face to face (Revelation 21-22). On that day we will experience His presence more fully than we have ever known. Just like Israel before us, we are the people of God on a journey to His presence.

The psalm tells in vivid detail about the journey that lay ahead. The journey was not easy, and ours is not as well. The barren deserts of suffering threaten us in just as real a way as the physical lack of water. But God sanctifies us through suffering, and not in spite of it. Suffering is the way that He so often transforms us into His own image and makes us what He has created to be. And yet, we can rejoice in the midst of our sufferings. This is a theme seen over and over throughout the New Testament (James 1:2-4, Romans 5:3-5, 1 Peter 4:13). We rejoice not because we enjoy suffering, but because God is with us in suffering. We rejoice because we know that God is working and we know that we follow the example of Jesus Himself. And from strength to strength, or from one degree of glory to the next (2 Corinthians 3:18), God is making us more like Christ. And what more evidence do we need that God will not withhold good from His people than the truth that He has not withheld His own Son from us (Romans 8:32).

So let us serve Him in whatever role He has placed us in. Let us rejoice in the midst of the suffering that He is using to strengthen us. Let us praise His name and live every moment for His glory.

HAPPY IS THE PERSON WHO TRUSTS IN YOU, LORD OF ARMIES!

Psalm 84:12

Day Four Questions

1. In what ways are our own lives similar
to the pilgrimage to Jerusalem?

2. How does reading this psalm from this side of the
cross deepen your understanding of it?

3. Read James 1:2-4, Romans 5:3-5, and 1 Peter 4:13. What do these
passages along with Psalm 84 teach you about rejoicing in suffering?

STEADFAST LOVE
and
FAITHFULNESS

This psalm is another of the psalms composed by the Sons of Korah. The psalm is a corporate lament, yet it is a lament with confidence. The people sing with sorrow over their sin and sin's consequences, but also with confidence that God will be faithful because that is who He is and it is what has been revealed through His Word. Much of the language found in the psalm is derived from Exodus 34 and specifically the description of God that is found in Exodus 34:6-7. It was in that passage that God revealed to Moses who He is and where we see our God as one who is both loving, compassionate, and merciful, and also holy, righteous, and truth.

Psalm 85 is titled in most Bible's with the heading "Revive Us Again." It is a song of mourning sin and its consequences, and a psalm of pleading for God to move. The psalm begins with remembering. The psalmist remembers all that God has done in the past when He was favorable to the land, when He restored fortunes, when He forgave the people, covered their sin, and turned from wrath. Then the psalmist moves from remembering the past to pleading with God for the present.

The psalmist pleads for God to restore His people, to bring revival, and to show His steadfast love anew. The psalmist longs for the people of God to rejoice in the Lord their God. Then in verse eight there is a shift in pronouns. The psalmist goes from speaking for the collective people to a personal plea. God's people long for revival, and it always starts with His individual people hearing His voice. So in one sense we could say that revival begins with individuals, but that answer would not be sufficient. Revival begins with God. It begins with God speaking and then His people can hear. He has spoken through His Word, and the book of Hebrews tells us that He has also spoken through His Son (Hebrews 1:1-3). Through the written Word of God we learn who God is, and through the gospel itself manifested in the life, death, and resurrection of Jesus, we see who God is and how He loves His own. God's glory "dwells in our land" because Jesus has come to dwell with us.

How can we describe the Lord? What words would be sufficient to describe who He is and all that He has done. Verse 10 of this psalm points to His character. He is the fullness of steadfast (Hesed) love, grace, and mercy. Yet He is also faithfulness (truth), holiness, and justice. Righteousness and peace kiss in perfect union in His person. For generations many churches have chosen to sing or read this hymn at Christmastime. They do this because they rightly recognize that it is through Jesus and through the cross that steadfast love and holiness stand in perfect unity. The apostle John would say it this way in John 1:14, that Jesus is "full of grace and truth." Though we often in our humanity find these exclusive or lean toward one or the other, Jesus is both. The sin of His people must be punished, so in love He takes that punishment on Himself. Grace and truth meet when Jesus hangs on the cross to become our substitutionary atonement.

The people of Israel had a perpetual sin problem. Year after year sacrifices would be made to atone for their sin. But all of those sacrifices were pointing ahead to one moment when Jesus would carry the sins of His people on the cross. The answer to the perpetual problem of sin is the cross. The cross is the place where love and justice meet. It is the place where salvation is completed. The cross is our hope for every day. And it is the cross that allows us to continue to pray for God to stir our hearts toward Himself.

HIS SALVATION IS VERY

NEAR THOSE WHO FEAR HIM,

SO THAT GLORY MAY DWELL

IN OUR LAND.

Psalm 85:10

Day Five Questions

1. What is the importance of remembering in this psalm and in our lives?

2. What do we learn about God in this psalm?

3. How does this psalm point us to the cross?

Week Five

MEMORY VERSE

For the Lord God is a
sun and shield. The
Lord grants favor and
honor; he does not
withhold the good
from those who live
with integrity.

PSALM 63:1-3

Read Psalms 81-85

PARAPHRASE THE PASSAGE FROM THIS WEEK.

WHAT DID YOU OBSERVE FROM THIS WEEK'S TEXT ABOUT GOD AND HIS CHARACTER?

WHAT DOES THE PASSAGE TEACH ABOUT THE CONDITION OF MANKIND AND ABOUT YOURSELF?

Week Five

HOW DOES THIS PASSAGE POINT TO THE GOSPEL?

HOW SHOULD YOU RESPOND TO THIS PASSAGE?

WHAT IS THE PERSONAL APPLICATION?

WHAT SPECIFIC ACTION STEPS CAN YOU TAKE THIS WEEK TO APPLY THE PASSAGE?

Unite My
HEART TO FEAR
YOUR NAME

In Psalm 86 we find another psalm of David. It is tucked in a section of Asaph and Korah psalms, and yet it's message fits perfectly in it's location. This is a psalm of personal lament. And though it appears to have been written in response to a specific situation in David's live, it is one that rings true for all of us. This psalm teaches us valuable truth about who God is and what our response to Him should be.

At the start of the psalm, David pleads with God for specific things. As He brings his earnest petition before the Lord, he also gives reason as to why the Lord should answer his pleas. The names of God that are used throughout the psalm are interesting to note. Though the psalm begins with the covenant name of God (*Yahweh* in Hebrew is translated as LORD), the most frequently used name of God is Lord (This is *Adonai* in Hebrew.). The specific choosing of the different names of God are very significant and understanding them helps us to understand the psalmist's message.

David begins by appealing to the LORD. He is appealing to God's covenant name. In verse two, the word that is translated as godly, could also be translated as loyal. This is interesting to note because David is using covenant language in his prayer. He is remembering God's covenant and pleading with God to keep the covenant He has made with His people. He is asking for covenant blessings for covenant faithfulness or loyalty. The blessings of covenant faithfulness are seen throughout the Old Testament and would have been familiar to those reading the words of this psalm.

But David also uses the name Lord. And this is the name of God used most frequently in the psalm. The name Adonai here means sovereign. And again, David is pleading to God on the basis of His name and His character. Just speaking this name of God in prayer was a reminder to David and to us as well that God is sovereign. He is sovereign over our circumstances and our suffering and He is sovereign over every aspect of our lives. This is why we can come to the Lord with confidence. We know that all His ways are good. We can trust that even a "no" is grace when given from the hands of a loving and sovereign God.

Petition is soon turned to praise as David brings his pleas for mercy and is reminded of His merciful God. There is none like the Lord, and David proclaims the praises of the one who has created and the one who sustains all things. David looks forward in faith to the day when every knee will bow before the Messiah King. And the words of verse 9 are echoed in Revelation 15:4 as praise is ascribed to the Lamb.

The prayers of David in this psalm are an example to us of praying the Word of God. David uses the vocabulary of Scripture to provide the vocabulary of his prayers. He recites to the Lord and to his own heart the steadfast and merciful character of God. He asks the Lord to do what He has promised to do in confidence that He will do it.

As we look at the words of this psalm we are reminded that it is Jesus who has walked the road before us. As we suffer in this life, we look to the One who has suffered for us and suffered without sin. We look to Jesus who is the embodiment of the covenant LORD and of the sovereign Lord. We see the attributes of God listed and the character of God on display in this psalm and we see Jesus. And in Him, we are assured that there is no suffering so great that could ever separate us from the love of the Father that is ours in Christ Jesus (Romans 8:31-39).

So with the psalmist we pray the words of verse 11. Father, teach us your way. Lead us in truth. Bind our hearts to your heart and stir in us a zeal for your glory.

FOR YOU, LORD, ARE KIND

AND READY TO FORGIVE,

ABOUNDING IN FAITHFUL LOVE

TO ALL WHO CALL ON YOU.

Psalm 86:5

Day One Questions

1. Paraphrase Psalm 86:11

2. What do you learn about who God is from this psalm?

3. David used the language of Scripture to pray. Pray through this psalm as you reflect over who God is.

WEEK SIX · DAY TWO · WEEK SIX · DAY TWO · WEEK SIX · DAY TWO · WEEK SIX · DAY TWO · WEEK SIX ·

GLORIOUS
THINGS OF YOU
Are Spoken

In the 87th psalm, we find another psalm written by the Sons of Korah. The heading above the psalm is also the title of a well-known hymn with its roots in this short but beautiful psalm.

Glorious things of you are spoken. These words are found at the mid-point of the psalm, and they are the theme of this song of celebration. The psalm is a celebration of Zion. The beginning of the psalm speaks of the holy mount and the city that is loved by God. Zion is beautiful and glorious not because of any intrinsic value that it holds, but because it is the city of God. It is glorious because He loves it. It is glorious because this is where God dwells. It is glorious because of God's presence.

But this psalm looks forward to an eschatological or future city. This is made clear for us as the psalm continues on. As verse 4 begins the names of nations are listed. The words of Psalm 86:8-10 that all the nations will come and worship and glorify the Lord is pictured again in this psalm. But the names of these nations are striking to us. Each one is listed in Scripture as an enemy nation. Yet here in the psalm, we see them listed as those that know the Lord. And not just as those that know the Lord, but as those counted among God's people. God declares that they were born in the glorious and beloved city of Zion.

The words should come as no surprise to us. From the early promises made to Abraham, God had promised that through the seed of Abraham all nations of the earth would be blessed (Genesis 12). And Israel itself was called to be a light to the nations (Israel 49:6). The Sons of Korah in penning this psalm, looked forward to a day when those of every tribe, tongue, and nation would come in to a new Zion and worship their Messiah. The words look forward to the mystery of the people of God made up of both Jew and Gentile (Ephesians 3:4-6). And they anticipate the day when those that were once outsiders are grafted into the people of God (Romans 11). They look forward to a people born not biologically into the family of Abraham but born of grace.

Through the power of the gospel a new people is made. Through the perfect life, substitutionary death, and the power of the resurrection those that were once far off are brought near. Outsiders become sons and daughters. And not just outsiders, but enemies are made heirs. Romans 5:10 reminds us of this truth, that while we were still the enemies of God and lost in our sin with no hope of escape, Christ reconciled us to Himself. This is the hope of Psalm 87; enemies and outsiders are made sons and daughters of God. That those once enslaved by sin are united to Christ through the power of the gospel.

It is no wonder that in the final verse of his famous hymn Glorious Things of Thee Are Spoken, that John Newton penned the line, "I through grace a member am." Because our status as children of God and citizens of a greater city is all of grace.

With the reality of this truth how can we not sing the praises of His name. He has rescued us when we were enemies. He has saved us when we were far off. He has made us His own and adopted us into the family of God.

"HE HAS *rescued us* WHEN WE WERE ENEMIES. HE HAS *saved us* WHEN WE WERE FAR OFF."

Day Two Questions

1. What made Zion so glorious?

2. How does this passage help you understand the mystery that Paul revealed in Ephesians 3:4-6?

3. In what ways does this psalm look to the future?

WEEK SIX · DAY THREE

Song
IN THE DARK

The final of the Korah psalms is another personal lament. But this psalm is quite different than any other hymn in the psalter. It is the only hymn that doesn't end with hope or an answer to the pain of the psalmist. The heading is "I Cry Out Day and Night Before You," and this summarizes the movement of the psalm. It is one of desperate pleading and sorrow and yet somehow it is also a psalm of worship.

The psalmist begins by addressing God with His covenant name and as the God of my salvation. Despite what the psalmist is facing, he knows who God is. He knows the covenant and He knows that salvation is from the Lord. He comes to the Lord crying out day and night. We are never told what the suffering is that he is facing, but we know that the struggle is ongoing and persistent. Yet his response is to pray through the pain.

The psalmist chooses to worship through the night. But this worship doesn't look like what we may expect. His worship includes the praise of knowing who God is and calling Him by His name. And this worship includes coming when coming is hard. It is coming with unanswered questions and tear-stained eyes. It is coming with the knowledge that God is good when our circumstances seem far from good. It is hearts laid bare before the God who already knows.

The psalmist came day and night because he didn't know what else to do. He asked and kept asking when it seemed no answers came. He poured out his heart in faith even when it felt that his prayers were hitting the ceiling. He wrestled with knowing that God is able to take away suffering with the reality that for some reason unknown to our human hearts, he is not taking it away.

The darkness shakes us – but it does not shake our God. Psalm 139:11-12 remind us that He is untouched by the darkness that blinds us. The darkness that sinks to the depths of our souls is like light to Him. And when the world sleeps and the tears flow, our covenant God does not slumber (Psalm 121:3-4). He sustains us through the night.

This psalm doesn't end with a quote-worthy phrase. It ends with darkness. But this psalm is not the end of the story. The story is pointing us forward to the One who will meet this desperate need.

John 8:12 speaks of Jesus as the Light of the World. And when the psalmist pleads with God in verses 10-12, wondering if God can work wonders for the dead, we are reminded that surely He can. The resurrection proves that there is nothing, not even death, that is stronger than our God. And while we wait in the darkness, there is nothing that can separate us from the love of God (Romans 8:18-39).

2 Corinthians 3-5 speak much of light and glory. But the glory that these chapters speak of is not a present glory, but a future glory. 2 Corinthians 4:16-18 reminds us that we must not look to the transient things that are seen, but to the unseen and the eternal. We must shift our gaze off of the temporary darkness and on to the eternal glory of the Son. 2 Corinthians 5:7 sums up perfectly the life of the child of God. We walk by faith and not by sight. We walk by faith when we cannot see. We walk by faith when the darkness draws near. We pour out constant worship when we feel constant sorrow. We rejoice in our sufferings because our covenant God is ever near. And darkness is not dark to Him.

LORD, GOD OF MY SALVATION,

I CRY OUT BEFORE YOU

DAY AND NIGHT.

Psalm 88:1

Day Three Questions

1. In what ways do you think that our separate pleading with God can also be worship?

2. Read and paraphrase Psalm 139:11-12.

3. How can you worship in the dark?

YOU ARE
FAITHFUL TO ALL
Generations

PSALM 89

Our last psalm ended in darkness and desperation. Psalm 89 begins in the light and overflowing with praise. It is still a psalm of wrestling and seeking the Lord in desperation, but it is a reminder to us that God is faithful in the darkness and in the light. He is not caught off guard by our circumstances and though it may appear that He has forgotten us, He never will. This psalm is noted as a psalm of Ethan and it is usually categorized as a corporate lament. Yet, it is a lament that is rooted in praise of who God is, as every lament of God's people should be. We grieve, and we mourn, but not without hope.

The psalm begins with worship. It begins with praise to God for who He is and the declaration of a desire to make God's name and faithfulness known in every generation. From the start of the psalm, the psalmist references the Davidic covenant. God's love and faithfulness to His people throughout Scripture is always displayed through covenant. Our God is a God of covenant and this is beautifully seen in His covenant with David that is found in 2 Samuel 7. It is there that God promised David to establish his throne forever and promised to build him a house. The house was not a physical house, but a lineage. It would be through this lineage that one day the Messiah would come, but when the promise was given to David, its fulfillment was still generations away.

The psalmist praises God for His faithfulness and greatness. The psalmist uses the covenant language of who God is that was found in Exodus 34. Our God is gracious and forgiving. He is faithful and holy. The psalmist proclaims God's mighty power and remembers how God has defeated the enemies of His people. All the world is His, and He is clothed in righteousness and justice. The psalmist sings of the blessing it is to be a part of God's people, and the strength that is found in His name.

The second half of the psalm lists out the the promises of God and the things that He will do. Over and over the phrase "I will" is used to speak of the things that the Lord Himself will do. He will crush the enemies. He will establish His throne forever. He will be faithful. He will keep His promises.

But then comes verse 38, and the tone of the psalm shifts. After the glorious praise and the recounting of God's faithfulness and the covenant with His people, comes the reality that the people are in at that exact moment. For all of the promises of God to His people, the people were weary and confused. From their perspective, the promises of God did not match up with their current situation. The nation was struggling. The king did not seem to be following after the Lord. The enemies of God seemed to be victorious. The cry of the people of God again was, "How long, O Lord?"

But God had not forgotten His people or His covenant promises. At the beginning of the psalm, perhaps the people thought that they were reminding God of His covenant promises, but in fact, they were reminding themselves of all that He had promised. And though in their present circumstances, they could not see how God could keep His covenant to establish the Davidic covenant, He would keep His covenant in far greater ways than they could imagine. The promises would not be fulfilled through an earthly ruler, but through Jesus Himself. The king that would sit on David's throne forever did not come as a military or political leader, but as a servant. While they were looking at the failures of human kings, a better king was coming who would keep every promise to His people.

We need to be reminded that God's ways are not our ways. We need to praise His name in the middle of the night when our circumstances don't make sense. We need to trust His ways when nothing makes sense from our human perspective. We need the true and better king. We need Jesus.

FOR I WILL DECLARE, "FAITHFUL LOVE

IS BUILT UP FOREVER; YOU ESTABLISH

YOUR FAITHFULNESS IN THE HEAVENS."

Psalm 89:2

Day Four Questions

1. Read through the psalm again and make note of every time God says "I will." What does this teach you about how God works?

2. How does this psalm remind you to trust the Lord when you don't understand what He is doing?

3. How should worship be a part of our waiting for God to work?

HE IS OUR

Dwelling

PLACE

PSALM 90

We end with the first psalm of the fourth book of the psalms. It is a psalm of Moses and it is a beautiful picture of who God is. It is a community lament that reminds us of who we are apart from God. Yet it also contains praise to God for who He is, and petition for God to move and work in our lives. As a prayer of Moses, it is likely that the words were prayed and sung by the children of Israel as they wandered in the wilderness after their redemption from Egypt. It is a psalm of longing.

The psalm begins in adoration to the Lord. The psalm appeals to the sovereign Lord as the dwelling place of His people in all generations. These opening words must not be skipped, and we must remember that these words were penned as the people wandered in the desert without a home or permanent dwelling. Yet in the midst of their wandering, it was the Lord who was their faithful dwelling place. With echoes of the garden temple of Eden and the present reality of the tabernacle that they carried with them came a reminder that their own dwelling place was in God alone. These words set the stage for the psalm that is to come. The Sovereign One is the shelter for the people of God set free from Egypt and for the people of God now set free from sin. For the people of God wandering in this world that is not our home, we must remember the Holy One is our home.

The psalm continues with lavish praise for the Creator God. The God who is our true home and dwelling place is also the eternal and unchanging one. The psalmist reminds us that though the Lord reigns from everlasting to everlasting, our human lives are like a vapor. Humanity is listed in sharp contrast to the holiness of God. While our lives our short and fleeting, He is eternal. While we are sinful and unfaithful, He is perfect in holiness and abounding in faithfulness and love for His own.

By the time we come to the twelfth verse of the psalm, the psalmist begins to petition the Lord with each verse. The psalmist pleads for God to teach us, to give us wisdom, to return and show us mercy, and to have pity on us. He asks God to satisfy His people, to make us glad, to let us see His work. And the psalm beautifully ends with a plea for the favor of the Lord to rest upon His people and for the Lord alone to establish the work of our hands.

What does this psalm that was written for those waiting and wandering in the desert have to say to us today in our own lives? The themes of waiting and exile are not isolated to the children of Israel journeying through the desert. Instead, these are themes that recur throughout the biblical narrative. And even near the end of the New Testament, we are comforted with the truth that this world is not our home and that we are citizens of a greater city. We are homesick for a city that we have never seen. And yet, He is faithful. The Lord our God is our steadfast dwelling place. We find our home in Him.

The petitions of the psalmist find their true fulfillment in Jesus. It is Jesus that is our teacher. It is Jesus who is the embodiment of true wisdom. It is Jesus who has extended mercy and grace to His own at the cross. It is Christ alone that satisfies the longings of our wandering hearts. It is only through Him that we can rejoice no matter what life brings. It is in Him that we are made glad as we find peace with God through the blood of His cross (Colossians 1:20). It is the work of Jesus that displays to us the glorious power of the gospel. It is through the cross and His substitutionary atonement that we find favor with God. And the works of our hands are purified and refined through the process of sanctification through the power of Christ alone.

This psalm, like those we have studied before, meets us in our need, comforts us with His love, grounds us in who God is, and lifts our gaze to Calvary.

LET THE FAVOR OF THE LORD OUR
GOD BE ON US; ESTABLISH FOR US
THE WORK OF OUR HANDS—
ESTABLISH THE WORK OF OUR HANDS!

Psalm 90:17

Day Five Questions

1. What do you learn about who God is from this psalm?

2. Read through the psalm again and record all of the things the psalmist asks of the Lord.

3. Make your own list of things that you are asking God to do in your own heart and life.

Week
Six

MEMORY VERSE

I will sing about
the Lord's faithful
love forever;
I will proclaim your
faithfulness to
all generations
with my mouth.

PSALM 89:1

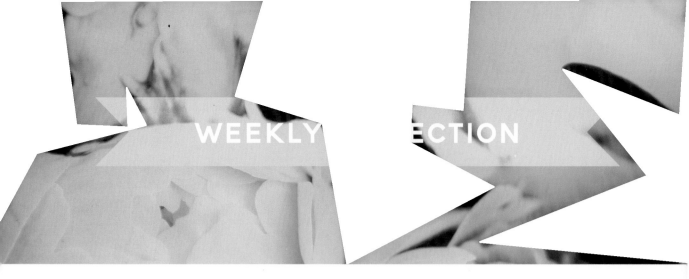

Read Psalms 86-90

PARAPHRASE THE PASSAGE FROM THIS WEEK.

WHAT DID YOU OBSERVE FROM THIS WEEK'S TEXT ABOUT GOD AND HIS CHARACTER?

WHAT DOES THE PASSAGE TEACH ABOUT THE CONDITION OF MANKIND AND ABOUT YOURSELF?

Week Six

HOW DOES THIS PASSAGE POINT TO THE GOSPEL?

HOW SHOULD YOU RESPOND TO THIS PASSAGE?

WHAT IS THE PERSONAL APPLICATION?

WHAT SPECIFIC ACTION STEPS CAN YOU TAKE THIS WEEK TO APPLY THE PASSAGE?

What is the gospel?

Thank you for reading and enjoying this study with us! We are abundantly grateful for the Word of God, the instruction we glean from it, and the ever-growing understanding about God's character from it. We're also thankful that Scripture continually points to one thing in innumerable ways: The Gospel.

We remember our brokenness when we read about the Fall of Adam and Eve in the garden of Eden (Genesis 3), when sin entered into a perfect world and maimed it. We remember the necessity that something innocent must die to pay for our sin when we read about the atoning sacrifices in the Old Testament. We read that we have all sinned and fallen short of the glory of God (Romans 3:23), and that the penalty for our brokenness, the wages of our sin, is death (Romans 6:23). We all are in need of grace, mercy, and most importantly: we all need a Savior.

We consider the goodness of God when we realize that He did not plan to leave us in this dire state. We see His promise to buy us back from the clutches of sin and death in Genesis 3:15. And we see that promise accomplished with Jesus Christ on the cross. Jesus Christ knew no sin yet became sin so that we might become righteous through His sacrifice (2 Corinthians 5:21.) Jesus was tempted in every way that we are and lived sinlessly. He was reviled, yet still yielded Himself for our sake, that we may have life abundant in Him. Jesus lived the perfect life that we could not live, and died the death that we deserved.

The Gospel is profound yet simple. There are many mysteries in it that we can never exhaust this side of Heaven, but there is still overwhelming weight to its implications in this life. The Gospel is the telling of our sinfulness and God's goodness, and this gracious gift compels a response. We are saved by grace through faith, (Ephesians 2:9) which means that we rest with faith in the grace that Jesus Christ displayed on the cross. We cannot save ourselves from our brokenness or do any amount of good works to merit God's favor, but we can have faith that what Jesus accomplished in His death, burial, and resurrection was more than enough for our salvation and our eternal delight. When we accept God, we are commanded to die to our self and our sinful desires, and live a life worthy of the calling we've received (Ephesians 4:1). The Gospel compels us to be sanctified, and in so doing, we are conformed to the likeness of Christ Himself.

This is hope. This is redemption. This is the Gospel.

He made the one who did not know sin to be sin for us, so that in him we might become the righteousness of God.

2 CORINTHIANS 5:21

FOR STUDYING GOD'S
WORD WITH US!

CONNECT WITH US:

@THEDAILYGRACECO

@KRISTINSCHMUCKER

CONTACT US:

INFO@THEDAILYGRACECO.COM

SHARE:

#THEDAILYGRACECO

#LAMPANDLIGHT

WEBSITE:

WWW.THEDAILYGRACECO.COM